30 Minutes Outside My Body

Martin Ndhlovu

Contents

Prologue

On Wednesday, May 6th, 2009, I died, while my lifeless body lay in bed, I went through the judgment of God, and God showed me a film about my life.

After 30 minutes outside my body, God allowed me back into my body.

This is the story of my life.

The sickness

I got sick on May 2008, my problem was I could not breathe properly, felt exhausted all the time, and had back pains. I went to several medical doctors for treatment, but there was no relief for me, instead of getting better my health was depreciating fast, and as a result, I could not walk for more than five minutes or do any work around the house. I would stay home most of the time and felt frustrated and helpless.

The doctors performed several medical tests to determine the cause of my sickness, but all the tests showed no cause for my illness. Some of my family members began talking behind my back, and some secretly thought I had AID, but no one dared to ask me what my sickness was. And looking back, had anyone asked me what was troubling me, I would not have known how to answer them.

And days and months passed, but I was not getting better. I could not sleep at night, sometimes, I had to get out of the house in the middle of the night because I could not breathe inside the house, and I would stay outside the house for hours until I could breathe normally.

Emotionally, I was depressed. I would consult different medical doctors, and every second day, I would go for medical consultation and the medical aid could no longer pay for my patient-doctor consultations.

It was not until March 2009 that a medical doctor referred me to a provisional hospital in Boksburg, South Africa. And the hospital did a chronic kidney disease test and diagnosis. The results showed that the right-side kidney was not working at all, it was dead, and although the left kidney was working, it was tiny in size [abnormal] and was positioned upside down, immediately the doctor at the hospital booked me for medical surgery with the medical specialist at Baragwanath hospital to correct the position of the left kidney. I had doubts and fear about the medical procedure to correct the position of my left kidney. I had read stories about people who have lost their lives while undergoing medical surgery to correct kidney problems. I did not want to die, for I was still young then, and had a wife and three children to care for.

As I had been in pain for a long period, I was becoming extremely sensitive and easily irritable, and being around other people was both tiring and depressing, and I was not particularly good company at that time. My wife must have suffered most as she was the only person with whom I spent most of my waking moments.

Many people offered many suggestions, and I bought many self-help over-the-counter medicine to an extent that our home resembled a pharmacy at the time. Looking back, if there is one thing am always proud of now, I have gained so much knowledge regarding general health and self-help medication.

But even with such knowledge of self-help medicine, I could not be cured and was beginning to despair. And knowing what was causing me to be sick was what frustrated and depressed me, for I knew that my condition was incurable.

Before I got sick, I was not a spiritual person, I had always believed that I was in control of my health and that with daily physical exercises, good vitamin supplements, and a good diet, I could live a long, healthy, and fulfilling life. I went to the gym every day; I was fit physically and healthy, and this was before I became sick.

I did not believe in God, I believed I was in control of my life and my destiny, but becoming sick, and not being able to do anything to cure myself, made me realize that there are things in our lives that render us helpless and powerless.

The strange thing about me being sick is that; pains intensified whenever I was alone. I do not know whether this was due to the stress of being alone and thinking too much. And as I did not believe in God, I began to suspect that I was being bewitched. This pushed me to seek help from traditional healers.

One traditional healer I consulted was a woman who was a librarian at the University of South Africa in Pretoria. I did not go out to seek this traditional healer for she was the one who found me. I had gone to the library seeking an article to complete my assignment [at that time, I was studying at the University of South Africa for a bachelor's degree in communication science]. I approached the information desk at the library for information about the article I wanted, and this woman [traditional healer] happened to be staffing the information desk at the time, she gave me the information about the article, but when I was about to leave, she asked me to wait a few minutes for she had some message for me from my ancestors, and she then ushered me to her private office.

In her office, she started telling me about how I almost died at birth, and how my ancestors had saved me from death. Not all she said was true, but yes, my mother did confirm that a medical doctor had declared me dead when I was a baby and that I miraculously came back to life.

The fact that the traditional healer revealed this secret convinced me that the ancestors are true, and this drove me to ancestral worship. The traditional healer later advised me against going for surgery to correct my kidney condition, for she said, "if you were to go for surgery your ancestors won't be pleased, and you are sure to die." I followed her advice and canceled my appointment at the hospital. And for a time, it seemed like I was getting better and had no pain. And this convinced me that dead people do have power, and I started believing that my ancestors had the power to influence my life for my good.

Outside my body

It was on Wednesday 6th of May 2009; I remember the day vividly as though it was yesterday. I woke up not feeling well, I was alone in the house. The children had gone to school, and my wife was at work.

I was sitting alone on the couch at 10: 30 in the morning, and suddenly a thought came to my mind that I was about to die. I have an elder brother who is a practicing attorney in the Empangeni in the province of Kwazulu-Natal in South Africa. I decided to send him an SMS [message] telling him to look after my family when I am dead.

I typed the message on my cellphone [remember those were not smartphones as we have them now], and when I finished typing the message, I pressed the send button on my cellphone, but to my surprise, the phone message read, "not sending." I then checked my airtime balance to make sure I had enough airtime to send an SMS, and I had R 27 airtime, and it was to send a message. I decided to press the send button once again, but still, the phone message reads, "not sending, I tried the third time, but still the phone message read "not sending."

I took this as an omen that I will not die, and I then decided to delete the message on my phone. Since I was not feeling well, I decided to lie down in bed for a while, and hardly two minutes after getting to my bed, I came out of my body. I cannot tell how it happened, I had no struggles getting out of my body, it just happened in a split second, it was like when you take off your clothes. I did not even become unconscious while it happened, I was awake.

Suddenly, I was out of my body, and I was floating in the air. I felt light, it felt like a heavy weight was lifted off me. And I could see my body lying on the bed, while I was hovering above my bed. I was surprised and confused, I did not know what was happening, for I had never experienced such a thing in my life, but at the same time, I felt relieved, for all the pains I had were no more.

And while I was staring at my body, a screen suddenly appeared on the wall of my bedroom, it was like a large flat-screen television mounted on the wall. And on the screen, I watched a play about me and the traditional healer [I had been consulting]. The traditional healer was trying to save me from death, but she failed, and then she ran away leaving me alone. When she was gone the play on the screen ended abruptly, then I heard a voice, but could not see the person who was talking, and the voice was telling me, "If you want to live, you must change your life."

At that time, I did not know who was speaking to me, I had suspected that it was God speaking to me through his Holy Spirit. Though the play on the screen was not long, not much about my life was shown on the screen. But God made me understand much about my life through his Spirit. I understood that God was displeased with how I lived my life.

Firstly, it was impressed upon my mind by God's Spirit that God was not pleased with how I had lived my life, particularly God was angry with me for consulting the spirits of the dead people [ancestors] and worshiping them. Secondly, God was angry with me for living a sinful life. I did not believe in God then, I did not go to church, and I did not even pray or read the bible. I had lived my life as it pleased me, this against God's will or law.

When God said to me, "if you want to live change your life, it meant that I had died already, for death is the separation of the body from soul and spirit. That I had come out of my body meant I had already died.

When I heard those words, "if you want to live, you must change your life," I instinctively knew that there were things that I had to change in my life and that I had to make the decision very quickly for there was no time for me to think about this since I was already out of my body.

I promised God that I would change my life, and as soon as I committed to change, God allowed me back into my body, and just as I did not struggle to get out of my body, I did not struggle to get back into my body, it happened also in a split second.

I think, I am privileged and favored by God, few people have gone through this experience and come back to life again. I do not know why God allowed me back into my body, am still struggling to this very day to fully understand the reason God gave me another chance to live again.

The reason God allowed me to live again has nothing to do with me, there is nothing good in me, I am a sinner just like all other people. God loves me and because God loves me, he decided to be merciful to me. God wants me to share my experience with other people so that they might know the reality of judgment that comes after death, every one of us will have to give an account to God about how we lived here on earth.

This agrees with what the Bible teaches, "then shall the dust return to the earth as it was: and the spirit shall return unto God who gave it. For God shall bring every work into judgment, including every secret thing, whether it be good or evil" Ecclesiastes 12: 7, 14.

The Bible says God created Adam's body from dust and breathed into his nostrils the breath of life, in other words, our physical bodies come from the dust of the earth, and our spirit and soul [which is the inner person] are from God. So, when we die, our bodies are buried in graves and dissolved into dust, and our spirit and soul [inner person] return to God.

I had always thought death was unconsciousness or endless sleep. I did not believe a person could live outside the body. And this out-of-body experience was a revelation. I now know and understand that the word of God is true, "then shall dust return to the earth as it was: the spirit shall return unto God who gave it" Ecclesiastes 12: 7.

At death, a person is broken out into two parts; the body and the inner person [the soul and spirit] are separated, and this refers back to how a man was created, "the LORD God formed man of the dust of the ground and breathed into his nostrils the breath of life; and man became a living soul" Genesis 2: 7.

God created man's physical body from the dust of the ground, and he breathed the breath of life onto his body, and at death, the two [body, soul, and spirit] separate. When buried in the grave, the body dissolves into the earth, and the spirit [the inner man] returns to God.

I experienced this separation of the body from the real me [the soul and spirit], that I could live outside my body, and that I could still think and speak outside my body, proves beyond doubt that what the bible says is true, we are born body, soul, and spirit. The body is the physical and visible part of a person, and the soul and spirit are the invisible and immaterial parts of a person.

Most people think that to die is to come into a state of unconsciousness or endless sleep, but far from it, a person is most conscious at death and retains all his or her faculties of the mind, emotion, sense of smell, and taste.

Had I not come back to life, I would not know what happens in the last hour when a person dies. I guess nurses and doctors at hospitals all over the world know more about death, for they have seen patients die at hospitals and cross to the other side of life. But even with such experience, they will not tell what happens as a person breathes their last breath, only God can tell us what happens when we finally die.

Recently, I lost a dear friend, she died of covid infection. She had been admitted to the hospital for two weeks, and while in the hospital, she was infected with the covid virus. The story of her last moment on earth is scary, it made me realize that what happened to me was real, not a figment of my imagination.

She died in the early hours of Sunday the 12th of December 2021. On Friday 10 December, she sends a voice clip, she was crying, and in the voice clip, she told me how two demonic spirits fought her the whole night, and how her spinal cord almost broke as a result of the demonic spirits' assault on her.

In the early hours of Saturday morning, the demonic spirit left her, and she was able to sleep the entire day. But around 9 pm on Saturday, she sent another voice clip, also crying, "she said, please pray for me, there are three demonic spirits, they have come to fetch me." she was desperately crying as she tried to resist the evil spirit.

I feel pain as I think about her death, she was a dear friend to me, we went to bible college together, and attended a home bible study for years. It pains me as I described her last hour on earth, but that I had to know the detail of her death is torture, but God had a reason why I should be privy to details about her last hour on earth.

Many things happen as people die, and we may never know what happens as people breathe their last breath. But my friend's story and my near-death experience show that the two worlds [the physical and spiritual worlds] meet at death. That we do not know or believe this does not mean that what I have said is not true.

While we live here on earth there is a veil that separates this physical life from the spiritual world. When we die our bodies get buried in graveyards, and our spirit goes forth to meet with God. So much happens in the spiritual realm that is hidden from our naked eyes, that we think life is all about what we see, hear, feel, and touch is a deception. This is the work of the devil; he works to blind us so that we will not believe and be saved. God removes the veil at death so we can see the next life. There was a young man who was infected with HIV-AIDS, and this young man was in the final stages of the disease, he could not feed himself, or even bathe himself, or even go to the bathroom by himself. He had to be washed and fed like a baby.

It so happen that as he was about to die, God removed the veil from his eyes, and in a vision, he saw of spirits of people who have died screaming in pain as they burn in Hell, and he saw himself entering Hell, as he was about to enter Hell the vision ended, and he miraculously rose from his bed, and rush headlong into the wall while screaming, "I will not enter", he banged his head so hard against the wall, the impact was so heavy that he lost most of his front teeth, and then he collapsed and died. We will never know whether his spirit did manage to avert Hell, for all we had was his dead body after his spirit, and soul left his body.

Death is a mystery to people who do not read the bible and believe in God, many people speculate as to what happens when a person dies, some even imagine that people return to this life in another form, and some think people become animals [incarnation], some even think dead people become gods [ancestors].

God tells us what happens when we die, God wants us to prepare for our deaths, life here on earth is temporal. We must think of this life as a transition or journey to another world. How we live here on earth will determine where we live in the next world.

Losing a loved one through death is painful, you know you will not see them, talk to them, or even touch or hold them anymore. When I lost my father in 1996, he died of a second stroke [he had high blood pressure chronic]. It was a very painful period in my life. I had never lost someone so close to my heart as my father.

I remember how confused I was when I saw his coffin lowered into the grave, I wanted to scream in pain, and could not bear the thought of seeing my father being put into a grave, and part of me did not want to believe that he was gone forever.

I knew nothing about death then, I thought my father was in that coffin, I did not know then that it was his body that was in the grave, and that my real father was gone to be with the Lord. My father was a believer, before he had his first stroke, God had warned him about what was to happen [suffering from stroke] even before it happened. And God also warned about the second stroke before it happened, my father knew three months before his death that God will take him.

"I would not have you to be ignorant, brethren, concerning them that are asleep, that you sorrow not, even as others who have no hope" 1 Thessalonians 4: 13. Sleep in the bible is used as the metaphor for death, if a person sleeps, there is waking up. A body of a believer rests in the grave, but his spirit and soul are in heaven.

I did not know death, for if I knew death, I will not have grieved uncontrollably for my father, now that I know Jesus will resurrect him when he comes back on earth, I have a hope of reuniting with my father in the future. People who do not believe the bible has no hope, for them, death is the end, and it is eternal separation from their loved ones.

My father was a staunch believer, he was a prayerful man, whom God has called into ministry. The reason God gave me another chance to live was because of the prayers my father had made for me and all of his children. Day and night, he will pray for his children without fail.

I am extremely fortunate to have been born of parents who know and believe in God, I think my background had been a preparation for a life of faith in God.

Prepare to meet your maker

As I was floating in the air and at the same looking at my own body, which was lying on the bed, suddenly a screen like a big television screen appeared on the wall. On the screen were two people, one person was me and the other was a woman [the traditional healer] whom I had been consulting about my health and other issues.

The Bible says, "for God shall bring every work into judgment, including every secret thing, whether it be good or evil" Ecclesiastes 12: 14. Sometimes we do things in secret, thinking since no one is looking, and nobody will know. But sadly, there is no private moment while we live here on earth. God sees everything we do, hears every word we utter, and knows our thoughts.

Every time you do something, be it good or bad, know that someone is watching and recording everything you are doing. I remember this story I heard as a child, "a man worked as a laborer on a farm. One evening, he decided to take his son along as he went to steal the maize on the farm. As the man and his son arrived on the farm [each carrying empty bags on their shoulders], the man told his son to check on his side and himself check his side to see if no one was watching them as they steal maize.

After checking and finding that no one was watching them, the man told his son to start putting maize in his bag. The son interjected, "father you say, we have checked all sides, but there is one place we have not checked. We have not checked behind the cloud to see whether God is watching us." With this, the father's conscience was convicted, and he decided that they should stop stealing.

As children, we thought this story was not true, and in secret, we have done terrible things thinking no one would know about. And as an adult, I continued living that lie, thinking I can do things that no one will know about. And having come out of the body and watched the play about my life, I now know that God knows everything we do, "O God, you know my foolishness, and my sins are not hidden from you" Psalms 69: 5.

God is everywhere at the same time, he is in heaven, and yet he is also present everywhere here on earth, "where shall I go from your Spirit? Or where shall I flee from your presence? If I ascend into heaven, you are there: if I make my bed in Sheol, behold, you are there" Psalm 139: 6-7.

If God does not see what we do or hear what we say, how can I account for the play about my life? Though not much about my life was shown on screen, there are things in my life I thought God did not know. Firstly, I worshipped the ancestors, and secondly, I consulted the spirit of the dead people and lived a sinful life.

This experience [out of my body] taught me that as we live here on earth, we must always be conscious that one day, we will stand before God every one of us to give an account of how we lived our lives here on earth. We always think that it does no matter what we do and how we live, I also believed this lie, when we die, we will rest in peace.

"They say, how does God know? And is there knowledge in the most High? Psalms 73: 11. The thought that God does not see and hear what people say and do here on earth is what encourages people to continue in wrongdoing. A thief or house breaker when he plans his crimes, always thinks that no one will see him commit the crime, and he will break into people's houses, steal, and get away scot-free.

That God does not immediately punish for breaking his laws, sinners feel secure, "because sentence against an evil work is not executed speedily, therefore the heart of sons of men is fully set in them to do evil. though a sinner does evil a hundred times, and his days are prolonged, yet surely, I know that it shall be well with them that fear God, who fear before him: but it shall not be well with the wicked, neither shall he prolong his days, which are as a shadow; because he fears not before God" Ecclesiastes 8: 11-13.

Once I was in the hospital ward praying for the sick in their hospital beds, and one elderly woman asked that she speak to me privately, the elderly woman had broken her leg while at home. She said to me, "young man, I love God, I read my bible daily, and pray daily. I do not steal or rob other people, I try to live in peace with people, and do good to other people. But why would God allow my leg to be broken, what sin have I committed? Yet there is this young woman who is always drunk, she passes by my house in the late hours every night on her way to her house drunk and singing, no one rapes her or troubles her, she is

20

healthy, yet am always sick, I suffer from high blood pressure, and am diabetic."

This was a difficult question for me to answer, for some time, I was lost for words, and I could not say anything in reply. I felt her pain and frustration, I was almost close to tears, but after composing myself, I said to her, "many things that are happening in this world do not make sense, the righteous people suffer, and the wicked people seem to prosper, and they do not suffer. But in the end, God will punish the evil doers, we Christians live by faith not by what we see, we know that in the end, God will reward us for doing good."

You do good as a person and expect blessing as a reward for doing good, but instead, suffer. This is an old problem as old as the world itself, "verily I have cleansed my heart in vain, and washed my hands in innocence. For all day long have I been plagued and chastened every morning" Psalms 73: 13-14.

A young lady asked to speak to me, "she said, I am a born-again believer, I live for God, and I try to live a holy life. I am growing old, women my age have their husbands, children, and houses. I have been praying every day and fasting [going without food] for three days every week. I want a husband, and children, I know I should get them in God's way, but am tempted to sleep with a man maybe, if I get pregnant, the man will eventually commit to me in marriage. I know this is against God's law but am frustrated."

How do you answer such a question? It is a difficult one. The woman eventually went against her faith and slept with a man out of wedlock, but she did not get pregnant as she had hoped, instead contracting a sexually transmitted disease [HIV-AIDS], and sadly, she died.

Not only do people think God does not hear and see what they do, but they think God does not exist, "the fool has said in his heart, the is no God" Psalms 14: 1. The presumption is the is no God, therefore we are free to do whatever we want, and this is also the reason people think the world was created by a big bang, because if there is no creator, people are accountable to no one, they can make their laws and govern themselves.

But my experience [when I got out of my body and God showed me how I lived my life in a film] proves beyond doubt that we will reap what we sow, "Be not deceived; God is not mocked: for whatsoever a man sows, that shall also reap. For he, that sows to the flesh shall of the flesh reap corruption: but he that sows to the Spirit shall of the Spirit reap life everlasting" Galatians 6: 7-8.

Mocking God means disrespecting him, denying his existence, and disobeying his law. The reason I wrote about my experience [30 minutes outside my body] is to convince you the reader about the reality of God and the final judgment. People have no thought of God, they do not think that God exists and that he sees everything they do and hears every word they speak, and most people do not think when they die, they will have to give an account of how they lived their lives in here on earth.

I once believed that I was accountable to no one and that I could live any way I wanted, that I could do anything I wanted, and that I was in charge of my life, 30 minutes outside of my body is about how God confronted me about my life, and now I am no longer deceived, I know that I have to give an account to God on how I live here on earth.

And if we know that one day, we will answer for the dreadful things we have done while living here on earth, we must live in fear of God. This fear of God will make us shun the wrong things, "the fear of man brings a snare: but whoever puts his trust on the Lord shall be safe" Proverbs 29: 25.

We do not care about how God expects us to live our lives, we are concerned about other people's expectations of our lives; we want to be loved and accepted by them; therefore, we will do anything to meet their expectations and gain their acceptance.

Fear of other people can make us do many strange things, Abraham feared that people will kill him for his beautiful wife, "it shall come to pass, when the Egyptians shall see you, that they shall say, this is his wife: and they shall kill me, but they will save you alive. Say, I pray you, that you are my sister: that it may be well with me for your sake and my soul shall live because of you" Genesis 12: 11-13. Therefore, Abraham lies and causes his wife to lie too.

And king Saul who was the first king to rule Israel, disobeyed God because he feared his soldiers, "Saul said because I saw the people were scattered from me and that you came not within the days appointed, that the Philistines gathered themselves together at Michmash. Therefore, said I, the Philistines will come down now upon Gilgal, I have not made supplication unto the LORD: I felt compelled, therefore, and offered a burnt offering" 1 Samuel 13: 11-12. King Saul did what only the priest was authorized to do, he offered sacrifice to

God, and he justified his actions by saying, the army was deserting him, and the Philistine army was gathered for war against Israel. And no amount of pressure either by people or our circumstances should make us do sinful things, we must live in obedience to God all the time.

A pastor was invited to preach before a king in his palace, and the pastor preached a message that displeased the king. And afterward, the king invited the pastor again to preach in the palace on condition that he would first offer an apology to the king for preaching a disrespectful message. The pastor knew that the king had the power to imprison him and take away his life, but this did not sway the pastor, instead, the pastor preached the same message he preached previously.

Before he started preaching, the pastor read a statement he had prepared, "I know before whom I stand this day to preach, the high and powerful king who has the power to end my life if I preach a message that will offend him, but my message is not from me, but from the powerful God who sees what I do, and hear every word I speak, this God has the power to kill my body and punish my soul in hell, this God, not the king, I fear most." After reading this statement, the pastor proceeded to preach the same message that offended the king.

After preaching the pastor sat down, he expected the king to order his servants to arrest him, but instead, something unusual happened, the king stood up and embraced the pastor, and the king said, "Blessed be God, for I have a faithful pastor."

Jesus tells us whom we must fear, "fear not them who kill the body but are not able to kill the soul: but rather fear him who can destroy both the soul and the body in hell" Matthew 10: 28.

The time comes for every one of us to make a choice, whether to serve and obey God, or to pander to the expectation of our family, friends, colleagues, friends, and even family can put us under pressure to conform to their expectations. Their expectations may not always be aligned with God's word or will; in such a situation we have to choose whether to conform to their expectations and disobey God or obey God and lose them as friends and family.

If we know that we will have to give an account before God as to how we lived here on earth and that God can punish us in hell for living a sinful life, we must choose to obey God. while you live here on earth, you are not alone, there are people around you, to support and cheer you up when you feel low, but whenever you stand before God to give an account of how you have lived your life here on earth, you will be alone, no one will be by your side.

Back in my body

After watching the film of my life on a small screen on the wall, God allowed me to make a choice, God told me, "If you want to live, you must change your life." I knew by instinct that I did not have much time to think about what God told me, I knew I had to decide there and there.

I told God I will change how I live, and as a result, God allowed me back into my own body. Sometimes I keep thinking, what if I had not decided to change my life, would I be alive today? If God had not allowed me back into my body, I would be dead by now, and no one would have known what happened in the last hour of my life.

I am grateful that I am alive today, I could have died almost thirteen years ago. On May 07, 2014, my wife gave birth to a healthy bouncy baby girl, her name is Tintswalo. She is a miracle baby, before we knew that my wife was pregnant, God gave me the name Tintswalo to call her, Tintswalo is a Tsonga name meaning grace.

Looking back now, I am convinced that my life is of miracles and grace. God has been merciful to me, and God has been my strength up until now, few people will go out of their bodies and come back to life. God had a reason for bringing me back to life again.

And this is the reason I have authored this book, my aim is that by sharing my experience with you the reader, I can convince you that God is real, and that judgment, hell, and heaven are real. The majority of people live in unbelief; they do not believe that God exists and that he will judge every one of us for what we have done and spoken while we live on this earth.

I did not believe that God was real, I did not even believe that the is life after we have died. I had always believed that death was an endless sleep. Whenever people spoke to me about the coming judgment, I always ridiculed them. More than a million people worldwide die daily, and I reasoned if a million people die in a day, how is it possible for God to judge every one of them? I also reasoned, if God were to judge every individual case, there would be a huge backlog of billions of cases to judge still to be judged.

Little did I know that what is impossible with people, is possible with God. God demonstrated this to me when he judged me for my sins within a few seconds in my bedroom [when I was out of my body for 30 minutes]. Now I know God is capable of judging billions of cases simultaneously in a second.

Before God revealed my daughter's name, my wife had gone for sonar and pregnancy tests for three months in succession, but all tests proved negative. When God gave me her name, it was on Friday, and my wife was on annual leave. I told her, God gave a name for a baby girl, you must be pregnant," she replied, I had done sonar and pregnancy tests for the last three months, and am not pregnant, but because you insist, I will go again on Monday."

27

On Monday, true to her words, she went to the family doctor and asked for sonar and pregnancy tests to be done again. The doctor was not pleased with this, he said, "you are not pregnant, for the past few months you have come here to do a senor and pregnancy test, but because you insist, I will have the test done again."

The test was done, and the test confirmed that she was six months pregnant. Everyone was surprised, it was indeed a miracle, she had not gained more weight and her stomach was flat, with no sign or even pregnancy symptoms.

Three months later, she gave birth to a healthy bouncy baby, her birth signaled a new lease of life for me. It was a sign of a new beginning for me and my family. It is also a confirmation that God is merciful to me and my family.

And ever since the birth of Tintswalo, I have been learning about God's mercy. God's mercy means that God does not deal with us as we deserve, he does not punish us for our sins.

God has been merciful to me; I could have died and gone to Hell. God did not allow me back into my body because I am good and live a holy life, am not different, I am like everyone. I do not always do good things, I have weaknesses and strengths, and I do not always do the good that I must always do for other people around me.

One day I had been reading the bible and praying for hours when suddenly it seemed like the roof of my bedroom had been removed, and I could see Jesus's face on the cloud. As Jesus appeared in the sky, he utters these three words thrice; "God loves you, God loves you, God loves you."

Back when Jesus had said this, I could not understand why God loves me, for I knew that I am a sinner like all other people. But now I understand why God said those words, God chooses people and saves them not because of anything in them, but because it is his sovereign choice, there is nothing in a sinner to attract the love of God and obligates God to love a sinner in return.

And back in my body, I have an opportunity to turn a new leaf, it is a new beginning for me. While in the past I had lived a sinful and selfish lifestyle, I did not pray, read the bible, or even care about other people. Now, most of my time is spent reading the bible, praying, and attending church.

Yes, I promised God I will change how I live, one thing I did change immediately was to stop consulting traditional healers [sangomas] and worshiping the dead, God is the creator and giver of life, and he alone is worthy of our adoration and worship.

It has been years since I had promised God that I will change, I have turned my life around, but I am still struggling with some old sinful habits and am not perfect as yet. But day by day, I am striving to be a new person. It is my habit that every day in the morning, I read the bible and pray. It is during early morning devotion that I feel connected to God and wish my whole life could be a life of devotion to God.

But as I man, I have other things to take care of, I need to earn a living and need to be around other people. This is where temptation comes, being with other people can be a blessing and a curse at the same time. In one moment, people can lift you, and other times they can put you down, or even tempt you to forget God and even do wrong, but we have to live with this, for God does not save us and take us to heaven when we become Christians.

Occasionally I yield to temptation and fall into sin, in my everyday devotion before living the house, I resolve to stay true to my faith, but this is not always the case, and whenever, I fail and fall into sin, I promise God, I will never do it again, but inevitably fail sometimes. But God has kept me in the faith, it is not because I am good and that has been a Christian for years now, it is because of God's grace that I have preserved the Christian life, "unto him who can keep you from falling and present you faultless before the presence of his glory with exceeding joy" Jude 1: 24.

Every Christian needs to be kept and preserved in faith until he or she dies, we live in a world full of sinful people, and as Christians, we are sinners who are saved by grace. We need to be preserved from outward sin, from neglect of duty, and from turning back to a former way of life [backsliding]. We have a sinful nature that constantly produces sinful desires.

God keeps us from willful sins, but with the conviction of his Holy Spirit, God keeps us from sinning ignorance by teaching us his word, and God makes us sorrowful and repents for our sins by punishing us for sins we commit.

Opening up about my out-of-body experience

We do not always understand everything that happens in our lives until all is passed. We do not always appreciate people in our lives until they are gone.

When it all happened [getting out of my body], I did not understand everything that happened to me at that time. I was confused and I thought that this was a common experience for every person.

We are slow to learn, for example, I did not understand how great my father was until he died, and I had to sit down to write his obituary, and put together pieces of information about his life, this allowed me to understand who my father was and a great man he was, I felt that I would not even measure up to his stature.

The same applies to my out-of-body experience, I did not understand everything about it when it happened and therefore did not see its significance. As I sat down to write about my experience, I am beginning to understand many more things about my experience now, than I did. God through his Holy Spirit is helping me understand more about this out-of-body experience I went through.

My wife kept begging me to share my experience, she thought this was something very special, and something that can help awaken many people so that they might turn to God and seek forgiveness for their sins before it is too late.

The other person with whom I shared the details of my out-body experience was a pastor whom God had told me to meet. I guess God sent me to this pastor for a reason, and because he had a personal encounter with God, he was better positioned to understand my experience and help me understand what I have just experienced.

One other thing that kept me from telling people about my experience was the fear of unbelief and ridicule. To most people, it would seem like I was dreaming or hallucinating. Most people fear death and avoid anyone who makes them think about the reality of death. People fear the judgment of God, they do not want to hear about anything that causes fear in their minds.

The majority of people were unlikely to believe and even understand the story about my experience and discouraged me from writing or even talking about my experience publicly.

I remember the first time I spoke in a public meeting about my out-body experience, I was a guest speaker at the conference of Assemblies of God church, and I did not plan to talk about my experience, but God moved me by his Spirit to share my experience.

I had an encouraging response from the congregation, people wanted to know more, and after the meeting, many approached me, as they wanted to know more about this experience.

The danger about sharing this experience is that it can be about me, and not about God, and a sense of pride may develop as people respond to my messages with praises, and I may begin to think that God saved me because there is something special in me.

Paul had an out-of-body experience, "I knew a man in Christ fourteen years ago, [whether, in the body, I cannot tell; or whether out of the body, I cannot tell: God knows;] How that he was caught up into paradise, and heard unspeakable words, which it is not lawful for a man to utter" 2 Corinthians 12: 3-4. Paul had many revelations and personal encounters with the risen Jesus, all those could have made him proud, therefore God had to keep him humbled, "lest I should be exalted above measure through the abundance of revelations, there was given to me a thorn in the flesh, the messenger of Satan to buffet me, lest I should be exalted above measure" 2 Corinthians 12: 7.

The temptation could be turning this out-of-body experience to be about me, it could be tempting to think that God saved me because he saw something good in me. Paul faced a similar temptation to turn all this [revelations and personal encounters with Jesus] into personal glory and greatness.

God, therefore, humbled him, some suggest that the "thorn in the flesh" was the problem with his eyes, the theory is when he saw a blinding light from heaven and became blind, thought God sent Aeneas to pray that he be healed, he never recovered his sight fully, although he prayed for many people and many people miraculously recovered from their sickness and diseases, God never allowed him to be fully healed.

I can easily be tempted to turn my experience into personal glory and greatness.

Furthermore, I could be tempted into turning my experience into a doctrine [teaching or God's way of doing things], and therefore mislead people, that is why in writing this book, I was cautious to balance my experience against the word of God.

I have used many bible verses in my writing to demonstrate that what I have written agrees with the word of God, for the word of God is the final authority on all matters of faith.

Why have I written the account about my out-of-body experience? I have already stated that I believe that God allowed me back to life so that I can become a witness to the truth of God's word.

I pray that the Holy Spirit will help you believe what you are reading and that the Holy Spirit will use this book to awaken every reader so that they could be conscious of their need for forgiveness and reconciliation with God.

I am grateful to my wife, and children for believing in me, I cannot stress this enough, we all need someone in life not only to believe in us but to support us as well.

Risuna [my second-born son] was instrumental in helping me make my dream of publishing a reality, he is responsible for formatting, the cover design of the book, and uploading the book on the online publishing platform.

Studying the bible

Bible study was part of our curriculum at school, but I never had any interest in religious study. In high school we were given a timetable; I remember how I always avoided going to religious classes. On many occasions, I tried to read the bible from the first chapter of Genesis, but I could not make a progress beyond just a few verses of Genesis chapter one. I could not understand what I was reading, and after reading just a few verses of Genesis chapter one, I will lose interest, and stop reading, even as an adult, I tried reading the bible several times, but I got discouraged for I could not understand what I was reading.

After God allowed me back into my body, something remarkable happened in me, I found myself reading the bible day and night. Since I was home and not working, I used to wake up at about 4 am, I will start my day with a prayer, then read the bible until about 5: 30 am. Then prepare breakfast for my family, and when they are done, I will take them to school and then drop my wife at her workplace.

My daily routine consisted of prayers and bible reading sessions, which I will do for the entire day until about 2 am the next morning. Then I will wake up at 4 am, start with my morning prays, and read the bible, I used to sleep only for 2 hours only.

I no longer enjoy watching television, or even going out and meeting friends. What I had enjoyed previously before I got out of my body, no longer interests me. Whenever I met with family and even friends, I often spoke about the bible, and many in my family and my friend were beginning to avoid me. They will say, I bore them for all I always talk about God and the bible all the time.

The feeling was also mutual because what they always talk about was a turn-off to me, for example, men will always talk about money, expensive cars, and beautiful women. Most people are only interested in material things and richness but are never interested in spiritual things.

The change in my attitude towards God and the bible was the reason now I could study the bible day and night. But when studying the bible, I was not alone, I had a helper. I had someone present with me, this invisible person will instruct me where to read the bible, and from time to time, he will help me understand difficult passages of the scriptures.

Back then, I did not know whom this invisible person was who instructing me about the bible, it is only now that I understand that it was the Holy Spirit of God who was teaching me the bible's truth, and this proves that the Bible is not just another book written by men, but the word of God, "but when he, the Spirit of truth, is come, he will guide you into all the truth" John 16: 13.

I have learned that God is faithful and true to his promises, God always fulfills his promises, and there are several examples in the bible which prove this, God warned the people [living in the times of Noah] that he will destroy the whole world, and true to his words, God did destroy the whole world, "God saw that the wickedness of man was great in the earth and that every imagination of thoughts of his heart was evil continually. And the LORD was sorry that he had made man on the earth, and it grieved him to his heart. And the Lord said, I will destroy man whom I have created from the face of the earth; both men, and the beast, and the creeping thing, and the fowls of the air; for I am sorry that I made them" Genesis 6: 5-7.

God always perform his promises, he threatened to destroy the entire world, and he did destroy the entire world with floods, only Noah and his family and all the animal that entered the ark we spared from destruction by the floods.

God hates sin [sin is breaking God's law] and will never fail to punish anyone who disobeys his laws. And according to the bible, God has also promised to punish sinful people and destroy the entire world by fire, "but the heaven and the earth, which now are, by the same word are kept in store, reserved unto fire against the day of judgment and destruction of ungodly men" 2 Peter 3: 7.

But many people do not believe what is said in the bible, and just like in the days of Noah, there is so much unbelief. I was once a skeptic, I did not believe that the bible was the word of God and did not think that God will judge anyone for their deeds, be they good or bad. We need to fear that the judgment day will come unexpectedly, "but the day of the Lord will come as a thief in the night; in which the heavens shall pass away with a great noise, and the elements shall melt with fervent heat, the earth also and the works that are therein shall be burned up" 2 Peter 3: 10.

God instructed Noah to build the ark so that he and his family will enter the ark and be saved from the floods, and God instructs us today to believe in his Son Jesus Christ so that we may be saved from the fire that will destroy the whole world, "for God so loved the whole world, that he gave his only begotten Son, that whosoever believes in him should not perish, but have everlasting life" John 3: 16.

All of us have sinned, no one is without sin [disobeyed God's law], and therefore we deserve to be punished. The punishment for breaking God's law is death, "for the wages of sin is death, but the gift of God is eternal life through Jesus Christ our Lord" Romans 6: 23.

I also, like everyone else has broken God's law, I deserved to die and go to Hell to suffer an everlasting burn from the fires of Hell, but God was merciful to me, even though I was already dead because I was out of my body, he allowed back into my body so that I could live again.

When God said to me, "if you want to live, change your way of life," he was giving me a chance to believe his word, and turn from my sinful way of life. God is merciful, he will always give people many opportunities to believe the good news and be saved.

We are told in the bible that Noah preached to people in his generation, the ark was God's way of not only saving Noah and his family, but of saving anyone who will believe the word of God, but people did not believe it.

God was about to destroy the cities of Sodom and Gomorrah for their wickedness, the angel told Lot to warn his sons-in-law about the coming judgment of God, but his sons-in-law did not believe in him, "the men said unto Lot, have you here any besides? Sons in law, your sons, your daughters, and whosoever you have in the city, bring them out of this: for we will destroy this place because the cry against them has become great before the face of the LORD; and the LORD has sent us to destroy it" Genesis 19: 12-13.

The Bible says, Lot tried to persuade his sons-in-law to leave the city and escape the judgment of God, but they refused, "Lot went out, and spoke unto his sons-in-law, who married his daughters and said, up, get you out of this place; for the LORD will destroy this city. But he seemed as one that mocked unto his sons in law" Genesis 19: 14.

Lot's sons-in-law thought he was mad when he told them to get out of the city of Sodom, even today, many people will not believe that God will judge every one of us for how we have lived in his world. They will ridicule and mock people who preach the word of God.

God is patient, and God is merciful, in his patience he does not always punish us the moment we sin, but in his patience puts up with us, "despise you the riches of his goodness and forbearance and longsuffering: not knowing that the goodness of God leads you to repentance?" Romans 2: 4.

God's patience and kindness are intended to turn us from our sins, but some people interpret this kindness as a sign of weakness on part of God, "who were formerly disobedient, when once the longsuffering of God waited in the days of Noah, while the ark was being prepared, by which few, that is, eight souls were saved through waters" 1 Peter 3: 20.

God waited for more than a hundred and twenty years before he could punish the world with floods in the days of Noah, the LORD said, my spirit shall not always strive with man, for that he is also flesh: yet his days shall be a hundred and twenty years" Genesis 6: 3. It took years for Noah to complete the work of building the ark, while Noah was building God was giving people time to repent and believe. The Bible says Noah even preached to people of his time, "spared not the ancient world but saved Noah the eight people, a preacher of righteousness, bringing in the flood upon the world of ungodly" 2 Peter 2: 5.

Before God confronted me in my bedroom [when I got out of my body and God showed me a film about my life], I never believed that God does indeed punish sinners, "because sentence against an evil work is not executed speedily, therefore the hearts of sons of men is fully set in them to do evil" Ecclesiastes 8: 11.

God had been patient with me for many years, from birth until I turned forty-one, I have lived a sinful life, but he did punish or judge me for my sins. God was merciful and patient with me. That God did not treat me as I deserved can only mean that God had been giving me many opportunities to turn from my sins and believe in Jesus Christ as my Lord and Savior.

And because God does not immediately punish us for our sins, we become more boldly and continue to do evil, and his patience with us is taken as a sign of weakness, "they say, how does God know? And is there knowledge in the Highest?" Psalm 73: 11.

I had always believed that God does not know what is happening on earth, because evil people prosper in their wicked schemes, and I had doubted that God has the power to punish people for their sins.

I have always been reluctant to write about my out-of-body experience simply because I know some people will not believe what I wrote, and some will even ridicule me for this book. My wife has been nagging me for years, she believes that writing and telling people about my experience will help awaken people to the reality of judgment, so that they may seek God, turn from their sins, and be saved.

But if people cannot believe what the bible says, what are the chances that they will believe this book you are reading? When the rich man asked Abraham to send Lazarus to his father's home, to tell his five brothers about Hell and suffering, Abraham replied, "even if some were to rise from death, and go to the rich's man family to tell them about Hell and suffering, they will not believe."

God is patient, and he will put up with us for a long time, but there is a limit to even patience, you may never know when God has decided that it is time that you should be punished for your sins. I had an opportunity to hear the word of God preached many times. I heard people warn me of God's judgment, but my heart was hardened, and I resisted God's call and his offer of mercy in Christ.

Going to church for the first time

One Saturday morning the Holy Spirit spoke to me, this was six months after God had allowed me back into my body. For six months, I had been home praying and reading the bible day and night. The Holy Spirit told me that I should go to a church nearby and meet the pastor of that church and that this pastor will tell me exactly whom I was [meaning what role God had called me for within the body of Christ].

For years, I had not been in church, yes as a child I have gone to church on the instruction of my parents, but as a teenager, I became rebellious and developed a strong dislike for the church. And after so many years of not going to church, going to church, and attending seemed like the first time.

I still remember the first sermon I heard that day, the pastor have been preaching about Lazarus and the rich man. At the end of the sermon, the pastor made an altar call, I decided to go. I remember fourteen other people responded to the altar call that Sunday and the pastor prayed over us, and at the end, each of us was assigned a counselor who was to guide us in our walk with God.

I was assigned to a man who was the same age as I was, the man was not particularly good at communication, and he looked down on people. I briefly told him my story, how I came out of my body, and that God has shown me a film about my life and asked me to change the life I lived.

The man was not a good listener, he seemed to think that I had been deceived by the devil and his demons, and he told me to go home and pray. I told him that the Holy Spirit had instructed me to come to the church and speak with the pastor. He answered that I will not see the pastor, since he was the one appointed my counselor, I should listen to him, and I should go home and pray. I insisted that I wanted to speak with the pastor still. He answered, "the pastor will not be of much help to you, spiritually, he said, he was more mature than the pastor since he came to the Lord years before the pastor.

While he was still speaking, the Holy Spirit spoke again, he said, when God first called Samuel, Samuel did not know who called him, I remember this bible story because I have read it a few weeks ago, "the LORD called Samuel: and he answered, here am I. And he runs unto Eli, and said, Here am I; for you called me. And he said, "I called not; lie down. He went and lay down. And the LORD called yet again, Samuel. And Samuel arose and went to Eli, and said, "Here am I; for you did call me. And he answered, I called not, my son; lie down again. Now Samuel did not know the LORD, neither was the word of the LORD yet revealed unto him. And the LORD called Samuel again the third time. And he arose and went to Eli, and said, Here am I; for you did call me. And Eli perceived that the LORD has called the child. Therefore, Eli said unto Samuel, Go, lie down: and it shall be, if he calls you, that you shall say, Speak, LORD; for your servant hears, So Samuel went and lay down in his place" 1 Samuel 3: 3-9.

God called Samuel, but Samuel thought Eli had called him, Samuel did not know it was God who had called him. And here I was having been called by the Lord, yet like Samuel, I was confused and not sure who called me, God had sent me to this pastor so that he should guide and help me understand my calling. But the way this counselor was not helpful at all. I told him that God has called me, and he replied, "if God has called you, you would know God called, you are not called by God, but you are under demonic influence, go home, fast and pray, and come back to me and I will pray with you."

Sensing that we were not making any headway, I insisted that I will speak directly to the senior pastor henceforth, I told him, "You do not know what you are talking about, and you are not helpful to me." I went straight to the pastor's secretary and made the appointment for a meeting, and I was granted an appointment to meet with the pastor.

A few days later, I met with pastor Mulaudzi of Rock of salvation church in Soweto Meadowlands, he was very friendly, and helpful. He apologized for the way the church counselor had treated me. He told me, yes God has called you and he will use you mightily, but between now and your destiny, there is a gap, you need to learn much and be guided by him.

I will forever be grateful for the guidance, and even the mentoring of Pastor Mulaudzi, he had a huge library in his office, and he selected a book on grace, gave it to me, and said, "read this book, and once your finish brings it back and we will discuss what you read."

I was used to reading for I have been reading the bible day and night, and it did not take much time for me to complete reading the book, I was very much thirsty for knowledge. I took the book back to pastor Mulaudzi and he was very much surprised that I had completed reading the book in such a brief time. We discussed grace, and at the end, he gave me another book, this book was about chapter seventeen of John's gospel. And this was to be the pattern of our interactions, pastor Mulaudzi would give me a book to read, I will read the book, come back to him, and we will discuss what I read, and he will then give me another book to read.

I was learning much, and gaining so much knowledge of the bible, and soon I began teaching the word of God at home. My mother and my younger sister were the first people I taught the bible. And the night before visiting my mother in Dawn Park, Boksburg, God will always give the word to share with her and my sister who stayed with her. They enjoyed the lessons so much, and they were revived spiritually.

And at the church where my mother and sister fellowship, they noticed the joy and peace in my mother, and asked, "why are you so happy and peaceful nowadays?" my mother told them of the bible lessons, I have been giving her and my sister bible lessons at home, and they asked her if she will not invite me to come and teach at the church.

That was an opening for me to teach the word of God in the church. I had never taught a group of people before, and I was excited and fearful at the same time. The first time I stood in a pulpit I was extremely nervous and shaky, but it all went well, and from that day onward, every Sunday, I preached at that church, and God has been opening doors for me to teach and preach the bible to people.

For the past two years, I have been teaching the bible at Mayfair Baptist college. I studied theology at this college and later become a lecturer at the same college. I must thank Pastor Willy Dangler for allowing me to learn theology and for mentoring me. He has been a profound influence in my life, I will forever be grateful for his contribution to shaping and helping me grow spiritually.

A changed life

I promised God I will change my life, and I thought it was an easy thing to do, I did not understand then it will be challenging work and require continuous effort. I had a list of does and don'ts, and true to my promise to God, I did change my life. There were things I enjoyed like going to nightclubs, and drinking alcohol, those were easy to do away with. But other habits were exceedingly difficult to change and am still struggling even to this day to rid my life of those bad habits.

To change my life, I had to change my mind. Previously I have always thought life was all about me, and that I must be happy and have every good thing I wanted, I felt that life has pandered to my every need and wants.

I did not acknowledge that God had authority over my life, I lived for myself, I was the manager of my life, and I could do anything I wanted, and no one had the right to tell me how to live my life. I had to first acknowledge God's claim over my life to change it. And this was hard for I lived independently of God for years, to submit to him, to his laws, and worship him was going to be challenging work. For they say, "old habits are hard to break."

With time, I also learned it is much easier to change what I do than to change how I think and feel. Sinning is not just doing evil things but also thinking evil thoughts. We sin not just by

48

doing dreadful things, but also by not doing the good we are supposed to do.

And because I could rid my life of some dreadful things, I started thinking I was better than others, and that God chose me because I was better than others, pride and a self-righteous attitude soon developed in me. I remember a manuscript I had written, titled "why only a few people will enter heaven." I completed the manuscript, but never got to publish it.

One evening I attended a conference at the church, and the guest speaker was Dr. Eva Seobi, she is a medical doctor and renowned public speaker, God used her to guide me, and she does not even know about the powerful impact her preaching had on me to this day. And as she got on the pulpit, she said, "I have a message for someone here in the church. God says, "you are writing a book, keep writing, and at the right time, God will give you something to write about. I did not know what this meant, but deep in my spirit, I had a conviction that the message was for me.

After completing the manuscript, I looked forward to publishing it with excitement, but one evening after having finished teaching at the home cell, the Holy Spirit told me, "You will not publish the book [why few people will enter heaven]," but instead this is the title of the book; the two fountain heads, write you will publish." I was shattered emotionally, it had taken me months to write the manuscript, and my children and wife were also excited about the prospects of me publishing a book.

I did not disclose what the Holy Spirit had told me for fear of disappointing my family, I reasoned that they would think, I am confused and lacked ambition, why should I write a manuscript and after completing it decides not to publish it? I decided to start writing the new manuscript titled "the two fountain heads" in secret thinking I could complete it in a short time before they even notice it. And it was only after the Holy Spirit had told me, you will not publish a book titled "why only a few people will enter heaven" that I finally understood Dr. Eva Shobi's message.

I experienced what they called writer's block, and I could not write more than a page of the new manuscript titled "the two fountain heads." I was shattered emotionally, I thought the ambition to publish a book was gone, and I could no longer publish.

When the Holy Spirit gave me the title "the two fountain heads" it was around March 2015, but it had taken me more than seven years to complete the manuscript and have it published. But it has also taken me more than seven years to finally understand why I could not publish the manuscript "why only a few people will enter heaven."

I had a self-righteous attitude then and thought I was better than other people and that God accepted me because of my changed life. I looked down on fellow Christians who were struggling with sin. I thought I was better than them, and that God accepted me because I lived a righteous life. And as I looked back, am even ashamed now of some of my writing on Facebook, they were written by a man with a self-righteous attitude.

"When he has come, he will convict the world of sin, and righteousness, and judgment" John 16: 8. We cannot know how sinful we are unless the Holy Spirit convinces us. By nature, we love ourselves, and pride will not allow us to admit that we are helpless sinners who cannot save themselves.

I believed I could do good and earn my way to heaven through what I did. I remember an interview I watch where one journalist was asking a Jewish woman why they think they did not need Christ, the Jewish woman answered, "we do not need someone to die for us, we can obey the law of God perfectly and please God." I used to think I could easily obey the law of God and easily enter heaven, but God through his Holy Spirit convicted me of my sins and brought light into my life that revealed even my hidden sins. Now am I always conscious of my sins and my failing, there is no day, am not disturbed or troubled by my failing to live up to God's word. Every time I pray, there are more sins to confess before God.

I am not perfect as yet, like apostle Paul, am always conscious there is still so much I lack in my life to make me perfect, "not as though I have already attained, either were already perfect: but I follow after, if indeed I may apprehend that for which also, I am apprehended of Christ Jesus" Philippians 3: 12. I am not what I was [before that 30 minutes out of my body], but I am not what I should be, God commands us to be perfect, "Be you perfect, even as your father who is in heaven is perfect" Mathew 5: 48.

If there is one person who knows me better than most people is my wife, I remember one day we argued, I do not remember what the argument was all about, but what I remember

51

are her stinging words. She said to me, "I thought God called you to work for him in ministry, but now I doubt God ever called you." In reply, I said, I will not defend myself on this, but God who called me will convince you that he has called me."

After saying this, I left her in the kitchen and went to the bedroom, for I thought the was no use in defending myself. Alone in the bedroom, I decided to pray, "God, you alone know me, you called me, I cannot convince my wife you called me, but you are the one who called me, so proof to her that you called me." Having prayed this prayer, I started reading my bible, and to my surprise, my wife knelt in front of me with tears in her eyes, and said, "am sorry, I said you were not called."

I accepted her apology, but I was puzzled why she had changed her mind so soon. I asked, "what made you change your mind about me and my calling?" she said, "something strange happened to me after I had said those words to you, I felt a burning sensation on my face and my chest, it felt like a burning in fire, and soon as this happens, I felt in my heart that what I said to you was wrong and that God was punishing me as the results."

I am not perfect, and my wife knows this, but I am not what I used to be, every day as I wake up in the morning, I pray to God that he gives me the strength to do right by everyone and that he gives me strength to resist provocation and temptations, and that he also gives me the wisdom to understand his will and the strength to live a holy life.

This is my prayer every morning before I leave home, but before midday, I must confess, I say and do things I know that are not God's will for my life. In South Africa driving on the road is exceedingly difficult, you will always come across drivers who break the rules of the road, and ignore the rights of other drivers, and I find myself reacting with anger most of the time, I know I should not be doing this, I should have self-control and be patient.

And later when I pray in the evening, there is so much wrongdoing and failure to confess before God, and though am not what God expects me to be, I am glad that am not what I use to be, every day, little by little, am changing for better. Christianity is like a journey and even like a race that continues while we live in this world and ends when we die.

A purpose-driven life

If we are to live right, there are two most important questions we should answer; the first is why are we here on earth, and the second is what is the truth? Before I came out of my body, I had thought I am here on earth to enjoy myself, I lived to party, I did not deny myself any pleasure, and my attitude towards life was exactly as the bible described it, "let us eat and drink; for tomorrow we die" 1 Corinthians 15: 32.

I did not care about anything or anyone, I cared only about myself. I did not think about God, death, and judgment day. My attitude was we live once, and we die once, so while alive I must use my time to entertain myself. I thought, why must I think about death? I reasoned that death comes to anyone, whether you are happy, miserable, rich, or poor, we all die and get buried.

I did not give the right answer to the question; "why am I here on earth?" Therefore, I did not live right. I was a product of my thoughts, in other words, my thoughts shaped the kind of life I lived, "for as he thinks in his heart. So is he" Proverb 23: 7.

In trying to answer the question "of why I am here on earth, I have begun on the wrong path, no surprise I was headed for the wrong destination which is Hell. I reasoned if God exists, he exists for me, I assumed he is here to serve me, therefore he is obligated to respond to my prayers and satisfy my every need. I thought life was all about me; my needs and wants. I was the center of the universe, and the universe revolved around me and my need and my wants.

If you begin a journey by taking the wrong road, no matter how fast you move, you will not get to your destination. Life is a journey, and when we begin life with the self as a starting point, we will never fulfill our purpose in life or even reach our destiny, heaven. Life is not about what I want or what should I do with my life, but it is all about what God wants me to do, we are in this world to serve God and fulfill God's will, not our will.

Life begins with God; hence the bible also begins with God, "in the beginning, God created the heaven and the earth. For by him were all things created, all things were created by him, and for him" Genesis 1: 1, Colossians 1: 16. God has neither the beginning nor the end, everything else begun in him, "for in him we move and have our being" Acts 17: 28.

God created the heaven and earth including people," the earth is the LORD'S, and the fulness thereof; the world and they that dwell therein" Psalms 24: 1. If I buy a car, it belongs to me, I control it, and I use it for my own needs. God created heaven, the earth, and people, all created things belong to God. He can decide how he wants people to live in his world.

God created the Garden of Eden and planted all kinds of fruits that were good for food. God placed the two people he had created [Adam and Eden] in his garden, and God had the right to tell them what they could eat or not eat in his garden. It was not up to Adam and Eve to decide what they could eat or not eat in the Garden of Eden. They were to listen to God, and not be driven by their taste buds and personal ambition for greatness.

God allowed us to be born in this world, we are his world, and were created by him, we are not to live in the world to please ourselves, but we are to live obediently to his will and please him.

God placed us here on earth to prepare us for eternity, this life is temporary, and death is the transition to the next life, not the end of life as many thinks. Death is the exit door in this life, we enter this world by birth and exit this world by death. It is either we die and leave this world and go either to heaven or to hell or remain alive till the last day of judgment. And at the end of this world, we will all stand before God to account to him how we use this life, life is a gift from God.

God gave us gifts and or talents, and how we use all those gifts and talents will determine where we spend eternity, there are two places we can go to, it is either we go to heaven, and be with Jesus, and enjoy endless blessings, or go to hell, where we suffer endless pain and torment.

And what is the truth? Most people believe the truth is subjective, it all depends on what one wishes to believe, and the assumption is that we are all rational beings, we chose what to believe and not to believe, and this is the reason many advocate freedom of religion. Are we free to make up our beliefs? We are not free to believe whatever we want. This is the truth we must believe, "hear, O Israel: the LORD our God is one LORD" Deuteronomy 6: 4.

Before I got out of my body, I wrongly thought I had the right to decide what to believe, yes, God existed, and God worked together with the ancestors [dead relatives] to control the world, one had to appease the ancestors to gain wealth. I had wrongly believed that most people suffer because their ancestors were displeased with them. I was putting the ancestors on the same level as God, for I was deceived, I thought the ancestors I had the power to grant favor and wealth.

There are no other gods, we have one God who coexists in three persons, yet one: God the Father, God the Son, and God the Holy Spirit. We have one God who created heaven, the whole earth, and everything on earth, including people.

So, if we have one God, what are we do to with this truth? "You shall have no other gods before me. You shall not bow down to them, nor serve them: for I, the LORD your God am a jealous God. you shall fear the LORD your God, and serve him, and you shall swear by his name. you shall love the LORD your God with all your heart, and with all your soul, with all your might" Exodus 20: 3, 5 Deuteronomy 6: 13, 5.

We are not free to choose whom to worship, we cannot make up our gods, there is only one God, and all else are a creature of God. People who lived in the Old Testament era thought they were free to choose whom to worship, so they made images of wood or stone and worship them as their God, though today, even though we do not carve gods out of wood or stone, nonetheless, we feel we are to free to worship what we want.

What is to worship? "To worship is to honor or show reverence for a divine being or supernatural power: to regard with great or extravagant respect, honor, or devotion" Merriam Webster dictionary. The Bible forbids the worship of any other things, be it animals, the sun, the moon, or the stars.

Today people worship material things, they may not do the ritual that demonstrates worship, but they love material things more than God and put them first in their hearts instead of God.

"No man can serve two masters: for either he will hate the one and love the other; or else he will hold to the one and despise the other. You cannot serve God and mammon" Mathew 6: 24. Money has power, it can compete with God for our love and service.

God commands us to love him with all our hearts, minds, and our beings. But when we love money, we cannot love God with all our hearts, minds, and our being. Money competes for affection, and once we love money, the love of God is displaced in our hearts, and becomes money becomes our god, as our money can determine the direction of our lives, people who love money devote their time and energy to getting money.

Pleasure is another competitor for our affection is the love of self, and the love of pleasure, "for men shall be lovers of themselves, lovers of pleasure more than lovers of God" 2 Timothy 3: 3, 4. God has defined our purpose in life in these two commands love the Lord you're your God with all your heart, all your mind, and all your soul, and love your neighbor as yourself." But we fail to fulfill God's intention for our lives because of loving ourselves and loving pleasure. God's intent for the people created is that they should love God and love other people, but self-love and the love of pleasure can clog the love of God and other people.

Self-love is inward-focused, and self-consumed, if you focus on yourself, you will always be looking to benefit in your relationship with God and other people, you have this attitude, "what is in for me." You will regard God and other people as instruments to aid you in obtaining pleasure and what you need. You will always be looking at what you can benefit from a relationship with God and other people.

Religious freedom is a subtle rejection of God, putting God on par with what he created. The truth is that there is one God, and Jesus is the only way to God, "Jesus said unto him, I am the way, the truth, and life: no man comes unto the Father, but by me" John 14: 6.

Jesus Christ is God's gift to the whole world, "for God so loved the world, that he gave his only begotten Son, that whoever believes in him should not perish, but have everlasting life" John 3: 16. And what we do with Jesus, will decide where we will live in the next life, either in Hell or heaven.

The first human sin was rejecting God and outputting the self in the place of God. God is the creator of the whole world; he has the right to demand that creation including people worship him. To worship God is to serve him, many mistakenly think that singing is the only way to worship God.

If only we knew that life does not end, that when we die, we move into the next world, we will change our thinking and attitude towards things in this world and we will reorder our priorities. I once thought this world was the only thing that matters, but now I have changed my attitude towards everything else, "I count all things but loss for the excellency of the knowledge of Christ Jesus my Lord: for whom I have suffered the loss of all things, and do count them but rubbish, that I may win Christ" Philippians 3: 8.

Where I once thought getting money and spending it to entertain myself and be happy matters, I have now changed my mind regarding wealth and material possessions. I now view life with eyes to the next world, "lay not up for yourself treasure upon earth, where moth and rust do corrupt, where thieves break through and steal. But lay up for yourselves treasures in heaven, where neither moth nor rust does corrupt, and where thieves do not break through nor steal: For where your treasures are, there will your heart be also" Matthew 6: 19-20. Earthly wealth and material possessions and money are temporal, but heavenly wealth is eternal, this life is temporal and transitional, but the next life is permanent. So, we must put our trust in God, not depend on money.

Serving God

The choice is between doing what I want or living for God and doing what God wants me to do. I cannot please myself and at the same time please God, it is either I do what I want with my life, consequently, displease God, or I please God and dissatisfy myself, it is either me or God, it cannot be both. God's ways are completely different from our ways, "for my thoughts are not your thoughts, neither are your ways my ways, says the LORD" Isaiah 55: 8.

We sometimes think God is like us, "these things have you done, and I kept silence, you thought that I was altogether such a one as yourself" Psalms 50: 21. We might not use stone or wood to carve God into our image today, but in our minds, we create a god according to our image and likeness, not the God of the bible.

Firstly, God has revealed himself through what he has created, "the heavens declare the glory of God; firmament shows his handiwork. Day unto day utter speech, night unto night shows knowledge. There is no speech nor language, where their voice is not heard" Psalms 19: 1-3. Creation reveals the knowledge and wisdom of God, creation also reveals his goodness, justice, and power. We can know who God is, we can know his person because nature reveals him.

Secondly, the Bible, which is God's word, the bible reveals who God is. God has not left in the dark so that we might search for him; he has revealed himself in his word and revealed who he is in history as he dealt with the nation of Israel.

Thirdly, Jesus has revealed who God is and what is God like, Jesus reveals God's personality. God is the Spirit and cannot be seen with physical eyes, but Jesus made God visible by what he taught and by how lived. If Jesus had not revealed God, we had no way of knowing his personality, God cares for and loves the people he created. Jesus is the visible representation of the invisible God; Jesus is a demonstration of God's love for the people by dying on the cross for our sins. If we are to serve God, we have to know who God is, and what he is like.

God created the heaves and the earth for his pleasure, "you are worthy, O Lord, to receive glory and honor and power: and for your pleasure, they are and were created" Revelation 4: 11. God created people and everything else including the world for his pleasure. God did not create people for their pleasures, we exist to serve God, and not the other way.

If we are to rightly serve God, we must first understand what God wants from us, and understanding what God wants us to do will bring about the transformation of our minds, "I beseech you therefore, brethren, by the mercies of God, that you present your bodies a living sacrifice, holy, acceptable to God, which is your reasonable service" Roman 12: 1.

God has not dealt with us or even punished us for our sins, "he has not dealt with us according to our sins, nor punished us according to our iniquities" Psalms 103: 10. But God has been merciful and good towards us, "do you despise the riches of his goodness, forbearance, and longsuffering, not knowing that the goodness of God leads to repentance?" Romans 2: 4.

God has been patient and merciful with us, and this calls for a response on our side, giving our bodies as a living sacrifice is the way to serve God, other bible translation reads, "reasonable way to worship him," worshiping God is not just singing, but doing everything that pleases God.

We worship God when we do what God created us to do, a bird brings glory to God when it acts as a bird or when does what a bird must do by nature; for example, making a nest. We worship God when we do what God created us to do, acting contrary to God's intent for our lives is sin, it is breaking the law of God.

We worship God when we use our God-given talents and gifts in a right manner, "having then gifts differing according to the grace that is given to us, whether prophecy, let us prophesy according to the proportion of faith; or ministry, let us wait on our ministering: or he that teaches, on teaching; he that exhorts, on exhortation: he that gives, let him do it in simplicity, he that rules, with diligence; he that shows mercy, with cheerfulness" Roman 12: 6-8.

"For even their women did change the natural use into which is against nature. And likewise, also men, leaving the natural use of women, burned in their lust one towards another; men with men working that which is shameful, and receiving in themselves that recompense of their error which was fitting"

Roman 1: 27. God created a woman for a man, and said, "a man shall leave his father and mother, and shall cleave unto his wife: and they shall be one flesh" Genesis 2: 24. God's design is for a man to marry a woman when a man marries a woman, a man does what God intended him to do, this is an act of worshiping God.

"Whether you eat or drink, or whatever you do, do all to the glory of God" 1 Corinthians 10: 31. Most people think serving God is working at the church or even being a pastor of a church, but serving God is much more than working at the church, serving God is doing everything including such things as cleaning or even cooking with the conscious that you doing it for the Lord.

Serving God is having the consciousness that God sees and hear everything you do, serving God is doing everything to our utter best because God expects us to excel in everything we do. We cannot separate life into religious time and nonreligious life. Some people think about God only when they are at church, or reading and praying in the morning, but when they are at work, at school, or with friends, they are not conscious of God, and they do not think about God. Serving God is doing everything with the attitude that we are doing it for God.

Before I came out of my body, I did not think about God, I had no consciousness of his presence, in fact, I never thought God sees and hear anything I said and did. I lived a godless life, and with no God, I had no one to account to, I could do everything I wanted to do, as long as it pleases me. But now I live with the conscious of God's presence, I know God knows my thoughts, he hears the words I speak, and he sees what I do.

I am not perfect, from time to time I do fail to live up to God's expectations and am disappointed and hurt by this. There is no time when I do not have failed to confess my failure before God in prayer. But I am not what I was, yes am not what I should be, but am moving forward, forgetting what is behind. If you keep on holding to the past, whether it be a past failure or even past success, you can never make any progress in your journey.

Before I came out of my body, I had no public speaking skills. I could not preach, teach, or even write, I could stand on the public platform and address a crowd of people. I remember the first time I was asked to preach; I was nervous and trembling with fear, standing in the pulpit at the church in front of the congregation, I was shivering with fear thinking they knew what I was going through, but to my surprise, after I finished preaching, they were singing me praises, they felt God was using me to minister to them.

God had been merciful to me, I could have died, but he allowed me to live, because of his mercy and kindness, I am alive today, and my life is no longer my own, I no longer live for pleasure or even to please myself.

The Bible says, "for the love of Christ constrains us; because we thus judge, that if one died for all, then were all died. We love him, because he first loved us" 2 Corinthians 5: 14, 1 John 4: 19. What motivates me in serving God is his love and mercy, because of his love and mercy he forgave my sins and gave me a new lease on life. He gave me another chance to correct the wrong things in my life and have a new start in life. Therefore, I no longer live just to entertain myself, my only purpose is to do his will and please him, this is my main priority now.

Seeking God while he is near

The Bible exhorts us, "seek the LORD while he may be found, call upon his name while he is near" Isaiah 55: 6. How often I heard the preaching on this verse, but I never cared to listen and seek the Lord. I always thought preachers were people who had nothing to do in life and people who were bored and spent their time annoying people because they had nothing to do with their time.

Seeking the Lord means turning away from a sinful life way of life and believing in the Lord Jesus as your Lord and Savoir. We are sinners, and no one lives right all the time and never breaks God's laws, in seeking the Lord, we come to God through faith in Christ Jesus, believing that Jesus died on the cross for our sins. Seeking the Lord also means seeking forgiveness for our sins and seeking a relationship with God through Christ Jesus.

There is a time when the Lord may be found, and there is a time when he cannot be found. The present moment, while we are alive is the only time when the Lord can still be found, but when we finally die, with our sins not forgiven, we can never find the Lord, beyond this life, in the grave, it is impossible to seek the Lord and have your sins forgiven.

I never sought God, I lived a sinful lifestyle, and never believed in God. I heard people preach about judgment day, but

I did not believe God will judge anyone, death for me meant the end of existence. So, I lived with this attitude; "let us eat and drink for tomorrow we die." We live once, so we must make use of every opportunity we have now to enjoy life and have fun.

Since everyone faces the same fate [whether they be Christians or not Christians], we will all die someday. I thought Christians were miserable people who were denying themselves happiness on basis of a lie [they believe that whatever loss or suffering they go through in this life God will reward them for the loss they suffered in the next life].

But the day I got out of my body, I realized that I have been deceived and that the bible is true. Getting out of my body for thirty minutes was a judgment session for me. I did not sought the Lord, and It was late for me to can do anything to avoid going to hell. I had lived contrary to the will of God, I had broken his laws, therefore I deserved to die, and going to hell to suffer meant suffering and pain, I had rightly deserved to suffer pain for I have lived contrary to the will of God.

God showed me the story of my life on a small screen on the wall, and it was all true, I was guilty as charged. But something unexpected happened, instead of me sending me to Hell, God said to me, "if you want to live, change your life."

Those are words I will never forget, those are words of mercy, instead of giving me what I deserved, God was showing me mercy, he was giving me another chance to live again, he was giving me another opportunity to change my life for good.

I never looked back, I took the chance God gave me, and here I am today, a changed man, though not perfect, striving to live a life that is pleasing to God. I am mindful that I have been privileged, God loves me, and that is the reason am alive today.

This is not how God works, the bible says, "it is appointed unto men once to die but after this judgment" Hebrews 9: 27. To my knowledge no one has died, gone through the judgment, and then come back to life. My case is an exception to the rule, many people do not believe that you go through judgment the very second you die, because no one has ever died and come back to life and tell people what happens a second after you died.

God brought me back to life again not only to give me another chance to start all over again but also to be a witness. I am alive so that I can warn people about the judgment of God, I am here to tell people, and to exhort them to seek the Lord before it is too late.

Once you died, you go through the judgment of God, am not sure whether or not God will play a film of your life on screen as he played mine, but I know this one thing, "for God shall bring every work into judgment including every secret thing, whether it be good, or whether it be evil" Ecclesiastes 12: 14.

You will have to stand before God to give an account to God of how you lived your life here on earth, and once you died, you cannot come back to life again, you will be gone forever, and your family, friends, and relatives will mourn you, they will grieve for you. And at your funeral, they will make speeches, and though they will say only good things about you, none of what they say will influence God to change his decision about your destiny if you are meant to go to Hell, you will enter Hell.

And as you stand before God the Judge, you will cry and ask God to be merciful and forgive your sins, but it will be too late.

When you finally die with your sins unforgiven, it will be too late to seek forgiveness, forgiveness is possible only while we live. A story is told in the bible about two men who died and went to two different places, one man went to paradise, and another went to Hell: "there was a certain rich man, who was clothed in purple and fine linen and feasted sumptuously every day: and there was a certain beggar named Lazarus, who was laid at his gate, full of sores. And desiring to be fed with crumbs that fell from the rich man's table: moreover, the dogs came and licked his sores. And it came to pass, that the beggar died and was carried by the angels into Abraham's bosom: the rich man also died and was buried; and in hades he lifted his eyes, being in torment, and seeing Abraham far off, and Lazarus in his bosom. And he cried and said, Father Abraham, have mercy on me, and send Lazarus, that he may dip the tip of his finger in water, and cool my tongue; for I am tormented in this flame. But Abraham said, son, remember that you in your lifetime received your good things, and likewise Lazarus evil things: but now he is comforted, and you are tormented. And besides all this, between us, and you there is a great gulf fixed: so that they who would pass from here to you cannot; neither can they pass to us, that would come from there. Then he said, I pray you, therefore, father, that you would send him to my father's house: for I have five brothers, that he may testify unto them, lest they also come into this place of torment. Abraham said unto him, they have Moses and the prophets; let them hear them. And he said, Nay, Father Abraham: but if one went unto them from the dead, they would repent. And he said unto him if they hear not Moses and the prophets, neither will they be persuaded, though one from the dead" Luke 16: 19-31.

Life here on earth is transitional, we are on a journey to eternity, it is either you go to heaven and be with Jesus, or you go to Hell and suffer pain and torment. But we are not conscious of this until it is too late, and we stand before God to have our destiny decided whether we will enter paradise or Hell.

A lady who recently come into our home bible study invited me to a special prayer meeting at her church, and I asked her, "what the special prayer was for? She said, "we are praying for our dead relatives who are in Hell, we are praying that God will be merciful to them, and forgive them their sins, and take them out of Hell into paradise."

This is a noble and worthy thing to pray for, but will God answer such a prayer? I also have pains for friends and relatives and even my family members who died in unbelief, who died with their sins unforgiven, and whom I suspect are in Hell.

We have this one opportunity here, we can only seek the Lord here on earth while we are alive, once we died, the opportunity to seek the Lord and have our sins forgiven is closed.

There is a breakfast radio show that hosts a medium for two days every week. A medium is a person who pretends to have a connection with our dead relatives. I often hear the lady [the medium] tell callers about the good news from their dead relatives, friends, and family.

If only our dead relatives, friends, and family could speak to us, I am convinced this would be their plea to us, "please listen to those who preach the word of God, never ignore them, or even ridicule them, for what they are preaching is the important and life-saving message, if you believe what they say, you will save yourself from pain and suffering in Hell.

I guess even if dead people were to one day come out of their graves and start preaching the word of God, no one will believe them. I also expect that not many people will believe what I wrote in this book, some will think, I am hallucinating [thinking I was dreaming about being out of my body, while in reality it never happened, I was just dreaming].

You can ignore this, for God created people with the will to choose, we have a right to decide what to believe and what not to believe, and sadly, many people believe lies, "there is a way which seems right unto man, but the end thereof are ways of death" Proverbs 14: 12. God will always treat you according to choices you make in this life, and your choices will decide whether you spend an eternity in Hell or heaven.

And sadly, we always chose to "live by seeing is believing" motto, people believe only what they see with their naked eyes, and what is not seen is not real. Noah chose to believe God, God told Noah that he will destroy the whole earth [people and animals] with flooded waters, though it had not yet rained, Noah believed that God will do whatever he said he will do, "by faith Noah, being warned of God of things not seen as yet, moved by fear, prepared an ark to the saving of his house, by which he condemned the world, and became heir of the righteousness which come by faith" Hebrews 11: 7.

People who lived in the times of Noah did not believe that God will destroy the whole world through floods, they only tried to enter the ark when the rainwater became floods, but they could not enter the ark for it was already too late, for God had closed the door of the ark then.

God has warned us in his word also that he will judge everyone according to their deeds, "for God shall bring every work into judgment including the secret things, whether it be good, or whether it be evil" Ecclesiastes 12: 14. But people chose not to believe what God says in his word [the Bible] until they have died and stood before the judgment throne of God, people pleaded and cried for mercy as they stand before God in judgment. People do not choose to believe and seek forgiveness, but they have the time and opportunity to do so now while they are alive, for when we die without having been reconciled to God, it is already too late to seek the Lord.

The Bible says, "Lazarus died and was carried by angels into Abraham's bosom" Luke 16: 22. But the bible is silent, it does not tell us who carried the rich man to Hell, reading other verses of the bible we can conjure up who carried the rich man to Hell. "Yet Michael the archangel, when contending with the devil as he was disputing about the body of Moses, dare not bring against him a railing accusation, but said the Lord rebuke you" Jude 1: 9.

Moses died as a punishment from God, God had instructed Moses to speak to the rock so that it produced water for the nation that he led out of slavery in Egypt, but instead of speaking to the rock as God commanded, Moses beat the rock with the rod, so as result God was angry with Moses, "the Lord spoke unto Moses and Aaron, because you believed me not, to sanctify me in the eyes of the children of Israel, therefore you shall not bring this congregation into the land which I have given them" Numbers 20: 12.

God was angry with both Aaron and Moses and as result, he did not allow them to enter the land of Cannan, instead, they were to die at the border of the land of Cannan, "I pray you, let me go over, and see the good land that is beyond Jordan, that pleasant mountain, and Lebanon. But the Lord was angry with me for your sakes and would not hear me: the LORD said unto me, that is sufficient; speak no more unto me of this matter. Get up into the top of Pisgah, and lift your eyes westward, and northward, and southwards, and eastward, and behold it with your eyes: for you shall not go over this Jordan" Deuteronomy 3: 23, 26-27.

The LORD only permitted Moses to climb the mountain and look at the land of Cannan from a distance, Moses was not allowed to enter the land. The devil must have concluded from this, that Moses belongs to him, and as result, he wanted to have the body of Moses because he thought Moses belong to Hell.

We cannot make up a doctrine from one verse of the bible, but the experience of many people as they die shows that what I say here is the truth. Earlier I wrote about a friend of mine who died in hospital, how in her last moments said that the "three demons came to take her as she died."

Her story is not unique, I know people who had similar experiences before they die. While others have not seen the demons before they die, many have told their friends and family, as they die, they have seen their dead relatives come to carry them to the other world. This mostly happens to those who worshipped the dead relatives and family, no dead relative or family member will come and carry your soul as you die, these are demons disguised as our dead relatives and family, I will not write much on this subject, my aim was just to show you the reader, that when you die, your soul and spirit will either be carried by the angels of God to heaven, or by the demons [the demons are fallen angels, who are under the command of the devil].

And in the last moments of your life [whether in a hospital bed or at home, or the accident scene, in a wracked car] as you die, if you see the angels of God come to take your soul and spirit, you are safe, for your final destination is heaven.

But if you see demons or your dead relatives or your dead family member coming to carry your soul and spirit, know that you are lost, because you are headed for Hell to suffer pain and torment for your sins. You cannot seek God then; it is too late to seek forgiveness and reconciliation with God.

"Today if you hear his voice, harden not your hearts" Hebrews 4: 7. Whenever you hear the word of God, it is God's message to you, it is God speaking to you through a preacher, do not ignore the message, you must believe what God says, it is about your eternal destination.

You can choose to believe or reject the message of God, but know this if you reject the message, you are hardening your heart, at first when you hear the message of God preached, it is easier to respond with faith, but as you refuse to believe, it will be harder for you to respond with faith the next time you hear the preaching of God's word.

God told Pharoah to let the children of Israel leave Egypt, but Pharoah refused to heed the word of God, he hardened his heart, but God also tells us in the bible, "but I will harden his heart, that he shall not let the people go" Exodus 4: 21.

God hardened the heart of Pharoah so that he refused to let the children of Israel leave Egypt, is this fair, was Pharoah not doing what the Lord made him do? God knew Pharoah will refuse to listen to Moses, therefore he told Moses not only what Pharoah was likely to do, but as a response to the decision Pharoah made, God will confirm Pharoah's decision by hardening his heart.

When you refuse to believe the Good News, God will also confirm your decision by hardening your heart so that it becomes hard, and this punishment is because you refused to respond by faith to the Good News.

Salvation is of God

Can I ask you a question, do you have a soul and spirit that will continue living after your body is buried in a grave or cremated? And let me ask you another question; where will your soul and spirit live after they are separated from your body? There are only possible two places where your soul and spirit may live; your soul and spirit may either be in Hell [where they will suffer everlasting pain and torment] or in heaven where they will rest in peace.

Unfortunately, not many people ever consider this question, and not many people ever think about life after death, yes many do plan for their funerals, they take out burial policies and life covers to cover the expenses of funerals, but not many think about life in hell or heaven.

Many people are ignorant of what happens after a person has died, they do not think there is life after death, and many are careless about their souls and spirit, and they only think about their bodies. They only think about how to fulfil their bodily desires. To them life is all about what they wear, eat and drink.

"Take no thought, saying, what shall we eat? Or what shall we drink? Or how shall we be clothed? For after those things do the Gentiles seek" Matthew 6: 31-32. People who do not believe in God and people who know and believe in God should differ in their outlook on life. People who do not know and believe in God centre their lives around food, drink, and clothing.

We should be more concerned about things that last forever, all other things will be destroyed or come to an end someday, this includes this world, "the world passes away, and the lust thereof: but he that does the will of God abides forever" 1 John 2: 17.

But we are careless about that which will last forever. We do not think about our souls and spirit, and what is temporal keeps us from focusing on what important and everlasting. The rich man from the story of Jesus was occupied with drinking, eating, and clothing that he did not think about his soul and spirit until he died.

Where will you spend your everlasting life? Every one of us deserves to die and go to Hell, for all of us have sinned against God [sinning is breaking the laws of God]. I also deserved to die and go to Hell for the sinful way of life I have lived, when for 30 minutes I was out of my body, I had died, and when God showed me a film about my life, it was a judgment in session for me, and God could have rightly sent me to Hell immediately, for my spirit departed my body and was already dead.

But God was merciful to me, he never treated me according to what I deserved, yes God is merciful. But that is not how he normally deals with people after they have died, he does not allow them to come back to life again, my case was an exception. I have not heard of anyone who died and stood before

God in judgment and came back to life again, do not put your hope on having an experience similar to mine.

God's offer of forgiveness is available now not after you have died, you must seek to have your sins forgiven, and be reconciled to God now, and not wait until you die. The Bible says, "seek the LORD while he may be found, call upon him while he is near" Isaiah 55: 6. When we have died in our sins [our sins not forgiven], it will be too late then to seek the LORD.

All of us have sinned, we have broken God's laws, and the punishment for breaking God's law is death. No one lives right all the time and never sinned. We sinned by doing things that God's law prohibits, and also by not doing good things which God requires us to do.

We have to be merciful to other people, and we have to love other people, but instead of being merciful, we are vengeful, we do not forgive, but instead, we pay people back for the pain or damage they had inflicted upon us.

Instead of loving other people as we love ourselves, we only love ourselves and neglect other people. Some people have no place to live, people sleep on street corners or in abandoned buildings, people are starving because they have no source of income or a way to earn a living and those people we come across on every street corner or mall, begging, we ignore them or condemn as lazy and good-for-nothing people.

You can live an exemplary life, be a good citizen, pay your rates and taxes, be a good husband or wife, and even be a good parent, but all those will never earn you heaven, no amount of good living can make you escape death and Hell.

Living a good and exemplary life will not make you earn entry to heaven either, there are many good people in Hell, who lived good lives and minded their own business, but because they did not love their neighbours as themselves, they are suffering pain and torment in Hell.

Yes, bad people are obvious candidates to enter Hell and suffer the pain of everlasting burning, but you can live a good life and do charity work, but still enter Hell. If you never believed and love the LORD your God with all your heart and soul, you will be lost and go to Hell.

God's law demands that we love God with all our heart, soul, and body, but we love material things more than God, we value only material possession more than God, and this is breaking God's law, and the punishment is Hell.

We are born sinners, our thoughts are wicked, imagine if there was a USB that could be plugged into your head and record every thought that ever came to your mind. Would you not be ashamed if people could read your thought and know what you are thinking?

After God allowed me back into my body, he gave me a gift that was a great source of discomfort. I would know what people are thinking, I could read their thoughts. I would meet some people in the street, we will greet each other, and they will say nice things about me like you are looking good, and you are enjoying life, and God bless.

They will say these good things to me, but because of the gift I had, I will know that they did not mean every single word they uttered. Instead, inside they will be saying things like, you are looking frail, you must be sick or even be infected with aids and there is no hope for you.

I begged God to take away this gift from me, knowing that people's thoughts and privileges are torture. I could not live with people knowing their minds, even the bible testifies about this, "God saw that the wickedness of man was great in the earth and that every imagination of the thoughts of his heart was evil continually. The LORD said in his heart, I will not again curse the ground anymore for man's sake; for the imagination of man's heart is evil from his youth" Genesis 6: 5, 8: 21.

We do not become evil and wicked as we grow old, but from a young age we are wicked, David says, "Behold, I was brought forth in iniquity, and sin did my mother conceive me" Psalms 51: 5.

We are all born sinners, and we have a sinful nature, as babies, we were never taught how to do wrong, sinful living is an instinct. Our case is hopeless, we cannot save ourselves, nor can we reform ourselves, "can an Ethiopian change the colour of his skin? Can a leopard take away its spots? Neither can you start doing good, for you have always done evil" Jeremiah 13: 23.

In the above-quoted verse, prophet Jeremiah is asking a rhetorical question and he expects a no answer, not a single person can change the colour of his skin, nor a leopard capable of removing its spots. So, no one can change his sinful nature as we are all born sinners.

Saving a person [that is changing the nature of a person] is the work of God alone, we can only change on the outside or reform our way of doing things, but we cannot change our hearts, "the heart is deceitful above all things, and desperately wicked: who knows it?" Jeremiah 17: 9.

The heart is the fountain from which life flows, if the fountain is polluted, the water that flows from it is polluted as well, "for out of the heart proceed evil thoughts, murder, adulteries, fornications, thefts, false witness, blasphemies" Matthew 15: 19.

Since we have evil hearts by nature, naturally our lifestyles will be evil as well. No one can change his or her heart, changing the heart is the work of God through the Holy Spirit, "a new heart also will I give you, and a new spirit will I put within you: I will take away the stony heart out of your flesh, and I will give you the heart of flesh" Ezekiel 36: 37.

By nature, we are unresponsive to God, we do not seek him, and we turn away from his word. God has to seek us first and give us a new heart that will respond to him, love him, and obey his laws. The new heart that God gives produces godly desires within us, the old heart was unresponsive to God and was the fountain that produced evil desires.

But what is salvation? Before we can define salvation, we look at its origin, where did salvation originate? Salvation originated with God long before the creation of the world and people, and what necessitated salvation was the presence of sin. God knew beforehand that Adam will fall into sin and thereby bring the whole human race into slavery to sin.

God planned to save people first from the guilt of sin [that is the penalty of sin], the power of sin [slavery to sin], the pleasure of sin [we love what is evil by nature], and from the presence of sin [that is sinful nature in us].

And how God saves us? Salvation is the work of God, as I have already stated it is the work of God through the death and resurrection of Christ, and the work of Christ is applied in us by the Holy Spirit. We get saved by faith in the work of Christ.

By nature, we love what is evil and hate what is good, most people may disagree with me on this point, but the bible is clear on this, all people love evil, this is because we have a sinful nature, and this sinful nature inclines us to love evil.

"Choosing rather suffer affliction with the people of God, than to enjoy the pleasure of sin" Hebrews 11: 25. We take pleasure in sin, and this is the reason it is hard to turn away from a sinful way of life.

"You love evil more than good and lying rather than to speak righteousness. You love all devouring words. O you deceitful tongue. How long will you love vanity and seek after falsehood? The LORD tests the righteous: but the wicked and him that loves violence his soul he hates" Psalms 52: 3, 4: 2, 11: 5. We love not only lies but hurting other people as well.

For God to save us, he must give us a new nature, "a new heart also will I give you, and a new spirit will I put within you: and I will take away the stony heart out of your flesh, and I will give you the heart of flesh" Ezekiel 36: 26. The old heart was wicked and was the one giving us the sinful desire, the new heart will produce within us godly desires and make us love good rather than evil.

This is where salvation begins, God does not save us from the penalty of sin before he saves us from the love of sin. God gives new nature that loves what is good and hates that which is evil.

God saves us from the penalty of sin through the work of Christ on the cross, we are saved when we believe that Christ died for our sins. God's law requires the death of everyone who sins [sin is breaking God's law]. God's forgiveness is on basis of justice, in other words, God cannot forgive us on basis that we are sorry for breaking his laws, and neither can he forgive us on basis that we promise to change or not do it again.

I may wrong a friend, and apologize to him by saying sorry, "I will never do it again," and the friend may rightly forgive me, but this is not how God deals with sin, "without shedding of blood the is no remission" Hebrews 9: 22.

God's forgiveness is on basis of what Christ did on the cross, he died, and people can live, he was separated from God on account of his carrying the sins of all people, and people can be reconciled to God because Christ was separated from God.

Christ was punished on the cross for the sins of the world [all people], and all people can be forgiven because Christ suffered in their place. Salvation is God's gift to undeserving sinners, we deserved to die, and go to Hell and suffer everlasting burning because we are guilty of committing sins.

There are two aspects to salvation; salvation is Godward and manward; God gives, and man must take what God gives. God's gift is in Christ, and for man to receive what God gives, he must repent and believe.

Repentance and faith are not the cause of salvation, salvation is the gift of God, but to be saved, repentance and faith are necessary, without faith and repentance, we cannot be saved. Repentance is changing our minds about God and sin, repentance is turning to God in faith, and it is also turning away from a sinful way of life.

Repentance is not the cause of salvation, yet a sinner cannot be saved without repentance, on our own we are incapable of turning away from a sinful way of life, for we are dead in sins and trespasses. Repentance, as well as faith, are all gifts of God, "when they heard these things, they held their peace, and glorified God, saying, then has God also to the Gentiles granted repentance unto life Act 11: 18.

And on our own, we cannot change our minds about God and sin, repentance [changing our minds about God and sin] is the gift of God through his Holy Spirit. A repentant believer sees things for what they are, sin blinds us, and we do not see things in their true light.

Repentance is also changing our minds about ourselves, sin makes the love of self, and it also gives a sense of self-importance. We love ourselves and feel proud of ourselves, but repentance changes all of this, it makes us loathe ourselves and thereby humble ourselves, 'Behold, I am vile; what shall I answer you' Job 40: 4.

And removing the power of sin is not removing the old sinful nature in a believer, the sinful nature remains in a believer and continues to produce sinful desires. This source of frustration and trouble humbles a believer.

Glorification is when a believer is given a new body, this completely removes the sinful nature in us, and this will be accomplished only when Christ returns to earth.

The reality of death and judgment

Caught in everyday life, we never think about what happens when we die, the question is do we cease to exist and become nothing? Many have theories about what happens after death. Some think we become ancestors who are powerful to influence the fortunes of our living families and relatives.

For example, some think that their dead relatives can bless or curse them, and as a result, many live in fear of dead relatives, hence they always do things to appease them. And others still think death is endless sleep, dead relatives sleep in peace awaiting the final judgment on the last day, where Jesus will resurrect all the dead people and raise them to judgment, and for this, they quote this scripture, "many of them that sleep in the dust of the earth shall awake, some to everlasting life, and some to shame and everlasting contempt" Daniel 12: 2.

So, does judgment come immediately after we have died? Or judgment comes on the last day when Jesus returns to the earth? Some people think all people sleep and there is no judgment until the final day. The Bible is the word of God, and what the bible says about death, judgment, Hell, and heaven is true and final, we should believe what the bible says.

According to the bible, judgment has already occurred, and is happening now and will be in the future when we die, or when Christ returns on the last day. Judgment is passed, "he that believes on him is not condemned: but he that believes not is condemned already, because he has not believed in the name of the only begotten Son of God" John 3: 18.

To condemn someone is to express strong disapproval about someone and to condemn is to say what punishment a person will suffer. God has already condemned all the people who heard the gospel message preached but refused to believe and has said, everyone who dies while in a state of unbelief will go to Hell. Judgment is past completed action of God on those who refuse to believe, on the other hand, those who hear the gospel message preached and believe will have already been saved, "verily, I say unto you. He that hear my word, and believe on him that sent me, has everlasting life, and shall not come into condemnation; but is passed from death unto life" John 5: 24.

We already noted that salvation is the gift of God to sinners, 'for God so loved the world, that he gave his only begotten Son, that whosoever believes in him should not perish, but have everlasting life John 3: 16. God made Jesus an offering for sins, 'God was in Christ, reconciling the world unto himself, not imputing their trespasses unto them; and has committed unto us the word of reconciliation. For he has made him, who knew no sin, to be sin for us; that we might be made the righteousness of God in him 2 Corinthians 5: 19, 21.

Everyone has sinned against God, and everyone has broken or disobeyed the laws of God, but those who believe that Jesus died for their sins, will not have their sin counted against them, "Blessed are they whose iniquities are forgiven, whose sins are covered. Blessed is the man to whom the Lord will not impute sin" Romans 4: 7-8.

God sent Jesus into this world to save sinners like you and me, Jesus is God's gift to sinners, God sent Christ Jesus into this world to die for the sins of all people, but if we refuse to accept God's offer of forgiveness, we judge ourselves.

Anyone who hears the Good News [the gospel] can either believe or refuse to believe the Good News, 'Paul and Barnabas grew bold, and said, it was necessary that the word of God should first have been spoken to you: but seeing you put it from you, you judge yourselves unworthy of everlasting life' Acts 13: 46.

The Jews were the first people to hear the Good News preached, but since they refuse to believe and be saved, the Good News [the gospel] has been preached to all nations of the world, but everyone who refuses to believe the Good News has judged himself or herself unworthy of eternal life.

What is eternal life? Does this mean the dead people who did not believe the Good News cease to exist? We have already said, death is the separation of the body from the spirit and the soul, when the body is separated from the soul and the spirit, it dies and gets buried in the grave, but the soul and the spirit of a person continue to live forever without the body.

Every one of us continues to live after we have died, but death in the bible also means life without God or being separated from God. We were separated from God when Adam sinned, everyone is born outside a relationship with God, it was Adam's sin that brought death and separation from God, "as by one man sin entered into the world, and death by sin; and so, death passed upon all men, for all have sinned. For as in Adam all die, even so in Christ shall all be made alive" Romans 5: 12, 2 Corinthians 5: 22.

God is now reconciling sinners to himself through Christ Jesus, everyone can be forgiven and be reconciled to God, God's offer of forgiveness is available to anyone, to receive God's offer of salvation, we must repent and believe the Good News.

But not everyone is willing to repent and believe the Good News, and when we refuse to believe the Good News, we refuse to be reconciled to God and we are judging ourselves as unworthy of eternal life.

Since we refuse to be reconciled to God in this life, we will not be reconciled to God in the next life [after we have died], the place for those who died in unbelief is Hell. Hell is a prison where those who died without faith in Jesus are kept. To be in Hell is to be away from the Lord. Those in Hell are separated from God now, but those in the lake of fire will be separated from God forever, "death and hades were cast into the lake of fire. This is the second death. Whosoever was not found written in the book of life was cast into the lake of fire" Revelation 20: 14.

There are books written in heaven, and in the books are records of what each of us has done since we were born, there is also the book of life, in this book is the name of every person who repents and truly believes in Christ Jesus as his Lord and Savior.

Let me try and illustrate this, you are accused of beating a friend, the friend goes to the police station to lay a charge of assault against you, you are charged with assault, and you get arrested, though your guilt has not yet been proven, you are kept in prison until your case comes before a judge or a magistrate to prove your guilt or your innocence. You stand trial, and after carefully considering the evidence by the prosecutor, you are declared guilty and sentenced to five years of imprisonment.

When you hear the Good News preached, either you believe and be saved, or you disbelieve and are condemned, "he that believes on him is not condemned: but he that believes not is condemned already, because he has not believed in the name of the only begotten Son of God" John 3: 18.

When you hear the Good News, you are put on trial, and if you believe, you are declared righteous, but if you refuse to believe, you are declared unrighteous and condemned. Judgment of God comes immediately as we refuse to believe the Good News.

People go either to Hell or heaven at death proving that they are already judged, heaven or paradise is the place where the believers go after they have died, and Hell is the place where unbelieving sinners go at death. If people were not judged immediately after they died, what can be the reason some people go to heaven and some to Hell?

Heaven or paradise is the place where believers go after death, "it came to pass that the beggar died and was carried by the angels into Abraham's bosom: the rich man also died and was buried" Luke 16: 22.

Before Jesus died, was resurrected to life, and ascended to heaven, the righteous people who had died were kept in a place called Abraham's bosom. This was the place of rest and comfort, in the story of Lazarus and the rich man, we are told that Lazarus who was a beggar was carried by angels to this place.

We are not told who carried the rich man to hade, hade is also called Hell, and this is the place of torment. From reading the bible, we can conclude that the rich man was carried by the devil or his demons [demons are fallen angel, who works for the devil, these fallen angels are under the rule of the devil], "Yet Michael the archangel, when contending with the devil as he disputed about the body of Moses" Jude 1: 9.

Abraham's bosom was a temporary place where the righteous dead were kept, this was because the blood of animals could not fully pay for the sins of the righteous people, however after Jesus died, as he ascended to heaven, he took also with him the righteous dead to heaven, "I go and prepare a place for you, I will come again, and receive you unto myself; that where I am, there you may be also" John 14: 3. At death, there is the separation of people, the righteous are in heaven waiting for the day of salvation, where their bodies will be raised anew. And the unrighteous are in Hell, where they are tormented day and night, there is no rest for them, on the resurrection day, the unrighteous dead will also experience resurrection and will be taken from Hell and be put in the lake fire where they will suffer everlasting punishment.

That some people go to Hell, and other people go to heaven, confirms that judgment is already passed. You might be thinking this is mere speculation, no one knows what happens after a person has died. The word of God tells us exactly what happens when we die, "it is appointed unto all men once to die, but after this the judgment" Hebrew 9: 27. That also there is a first and second resurrection proves that people are already judged, for, in the first resurrection, only the believers are raised to life. The second resurrection does not happen until thousands of years have passed.

The moment we decide to reject the gospel [the Good News], we have sealed our fate, and once we died, nothing can be done for us. We have judged ourselves unworthy of eternal life, we have rejected God's offer of mercy and forgiveness.

"There is a way which seems right unto a man, but the end thereof are ways of death" Proverbs 14: 12. A friend of mine died recently from covid virus infection, this friend of mine was a believer, she loved Christ, and she was very enthusiastic about prayer and bible study, at the beginning of every year, she fasted for forty days.

We thought she would enter heaven and she was an obvious candidate. But at the end of her life, there is doubt as to whether she made it to heaven.

We can deceive ourselves into thinking we are on the path that leads to heaven, but in the end, get lost and go to hell. Eternity or life after death is too important to be left to chance, we cannot gamble about our fate, and we should make sure that we are on the right path that leads to heaven. Judgment comes after we have died, and after we have died, our fate is sealed, it cannot be changed. If we have continued in unbelief and sin, the only thing that awaits us is pain and suffering in Hell.

Jesus described Hell, "shall cut him asunder, and appoint him his portion with the hypocrites: there shall be weeping and gnashing of teeth" Matthew 24: 51. Hell is the place where the hypocrites are assigned, a hypocrite is without the truth. Hell is a place of immense suffering and pain.

Hell is a temporal prison for those who died with their sins unforgiven, but when Jesus returns to earth, a more permanent place for those who died in unbelief will be the lake of fire. The lake of fire is a very terrible place compared with Hell, in Hell, it is only the soul and spirit of the dead that suffers, however in the lake of fire, people will suffer everlasting burn bodily.

Why are we here on earth?

If you do not know why you were born, you will never understand your purpose in life. Conversely, if you do not know why you were born, you are not likely to fulfill your purpose here on earth. If we begin with ourselves, we will never know why we are here on earth. If you want to get to town and you do not know the route, the navigator will get you there only if you type the right address, however, if you type the wrong address, no matter how fast you travel, you will not get to your destination.

If we want to know why we are here on earth, we must begin with God, "he died for all, that they who live should no longer live unto themselves, but unto him who died for them, and rose again" 2 Corinthians 5: 15.

Living for self-started when Adam and Eve fell into sin, the reason Eve ate the fruit from the tree of knowledge of good and evil was ambition for knowledge and self-promotion. "for God does know that in the day you eat thereof, then your eyes shall be opened, and you shall be as gods, knowing good and evil" Genesis 3: 5.

Eve wanted to decide for herself what was good and what was evil, the right to determine what is right and what is wrong belongs to God alone, and God as the creator has the right to tell them [Adam and Eve] what they could eat and not eat in his garden. And by extension, God has the right to tell us what we can do, and not do in his world, for he created us, and everything on earth, everything that is in this world belongs to God.

We are here on move and his pleasure, it is God alone who decided that we should be born, and it is him alone who is keeping us alive, "for in him we move, and have our being" Acts 17: 28. Without God, there will be no life here on earth, we owe our existence to God, therefore, we should live for him.

The right question we should be asking ourselves is not what I want to do with my life, but what God wants me to do with my life. Jesus put this bluntly, "if any man will come after me, let him deny himself, and take up his cross and follow me" Matthew 16: 24.

The choice is whether we will deny ourselves and obey God or deny God and follow our sinful desires. When we live for ourselves, we will always ignore God and break his laws. When we live for God, we will always deny not only our sinful desires but also our legitimate desires to obey God.

Who will you please, will you please yourself and ignore God? our eternal destiny depends on the answer to this question, if we ignore God and his laws, we will die and go to Hell, and suffer pain for breaking God's laws.

Before getting out of my body for 30 minutes, I lived a self-pleasing life, I did not deny myself anything I wanted, my desires were laws to me, and that meant even hurting others to get what I wanted. Sin is not just doing evil things but is doing what I want irrespective of whom I hurt in the process.

Many Christians even though they claim to be saved still live a self-centered life. They do not care about others; they are even ignorant as to how hurtful their actions are to other people.

You are here on earth for God to use you to impact the lives of other people, that is why the greatest command is this, "you shall love the Lord your God with all your heart, and with all your soul, and with all your mind. And you shall love your neighbor as yourself" Matthew 22: 37, 39. We do not love God and other people, instead, we love ourselves and material things. In the parable of Lazarus and the rich man, the rich man did not do anything bad, but he lived for himself, "there was a certain rich man, who was clothed in purple and fine linen, and feasted sumptuously every day" Luke 16: 19. He lived a life of partying and ignored the plight of the sick and poor Lazarus, this is what got him into Hell.

The rich young ruler chose material possessions and wealth over the kingdom of God, "Jesus said unto him, if you will be perfect, go sell what you have, and give to the poor, and you shall have treasure in heaven: and come and follow me. But when the young man heard that saying, he went away sorrowful: for he had great possessions" Matthew 19: 21-22. He was unwilling to part with his material possessions, for he did not love others as himself.

We live a self-centered life, instead of God-centered life. We depend on ourselves and our abilities, instead of depending on God and his provision. We affirm ourselves, instead of glorifying God. We look at things from a human perspective, instead of looking at things from God's perspective, "therefore from now on know we no man after the flesh, yea, though we have known Christ after the flesh, yet from now on know we him no more. Therefore, if any man is in Christ, he is a new creation: old things are passed away; behold, all things are becoming new" 2 Corinthians 5: 16-17.

And instead of seeking God and his righteousness, we seek what pleases us, and we live self-seeking lives, instead of promoting the interest of God's kingdom here on earth, we live selfish lives and promote only selfish interest.

The basis of God's judgment will be on whether we lived only for our selfish interest while ignoring the plight of the sick, poor, and destitute people around us, selfishness is what makes us ignore the sick, poor, and destitute people.

You cannot serve both yourself and God at the same time, it is either you become a master over your life, or God becomes your Lord. Either you submit to Jesus as your Lord and Savior, or you become the lord of your kingdom, it is either his kingdom or your kingdom, it cannot be both.

The final judgment will be on basis of whether or not we have obeyed God, as you live here on earth be mindful that one day you will stand before God to give an account of how you have lived your life on God's earth, "let us hear the conclusion of the whole matter; fear God and keep his commandments for this is the whole duty of man. For God shall bring every work into judgment, whether it be good or evil" Ecclesiastes 12: 13-14.

What the experience taught me.

At first, I was very reluctant to share my experience [my out-of-body experience. I know there are skeptics out there that will question anything they know nothing about. There are doubting Thomas out there who will not believe unless they have seen.

There are also thousands of people out there who will ridicule my experience on the basis that I was hallucinating, writing this book, I was mindful of such people. But I also know that there are thousands of people out there who will benefit from reading this book.

My question to all of you is this, what if you are wrong in your assumptions, and I am right? What if you find out late that there is indeed God who will judge everyone according to what they have done? Would it not be too late, when you are standing before God and are required to give an account before him of how you lived, and you find out that there was a way to have your sins forgiven and be saved, but now it is too late for you?

You have a soul and a spirit that will continue to live long after your body is buried and rot in the grave, do not be careless about your soul and spirit, there are more valuable that the body because they last forever. Can you endure everlasting burning and the resultant pain and suffering in Hell?

I was once doubting Thomas, I did not believe anything unless it appealed to my senses, unless it made sense to my mind. Since my out-of-body experience, I now live by faith, it is either you believe what the bible says, or you will experience what the bible says when you die, your body gets buried in the grave and your soul and spirit stand before God, to give an account of how you have lived your life here on earth.

The Bible says, "Jesus said unto him, Thomas because you have seen me, you have believed: blessed are they that have not seen, and yet have believed" John 20: 29. Thomas was one of the disciples of Jesus, he was not present when the resurrected Jesus first appeared to his disciples, they must have told him that Jesus was alive, yet he wanted to see Jesus for himself, he did not want to believe what other disciples told him, "but Thomas, the one of the twelve, called Didymus, was not with them when Jesus came. The other disciples therefore said; therefore, We have seen the Lord. But he said unto them, except I shall see in his hands the print of nails, and thrust my hand into his side, I will not believe" John 20: 24-25.

Many people are not willing to believe what the bible says, and Abraham said this of them, "he said unto him if they hear not Moses and the prophets, neither will they be persuaded, though one rose the dead" Luke 16: 31.

I have not believed the bible, and I did not even believe the testimony of those who called themselves children of God, I did not believe until I came out of my body, and God showed me the film of my life. I am grateful to God, not everyone has the privilege I have [to die and come back to life], I am one of the few people on earth to have such an experience.

I could have died and never come back to tell my story, but God has a reason for bringing me back to life again. One of the reasons is that I can testify about my experience and anyone with an open mind will believe and be saved. I pray that God may use this book through his Holy Spirit to bring other people to faith.

Whenever I come across a funeral procession or hear of the death of someone, the first question that comes to my mind is this, did the deceased have an opportunity to believe and repent? If the person who has died was not a believer, am troubled because I know they are suffering pain and torment in Hell.

In 2021 December a close friend of mine died, she was a believer, but the last recorded voice clip she sent from her bed in the hospital when she was about to die, is not giving me peace. I would love for my friend to be in heaven, but there is so much doubt as to where she might be.

And whenever I think about my younger sister, I am consoled, my sister died in 2017. Even today, her last word before she died, still rings in my ears, "I am very much humbled and thankful for the care you have given me; I misjudged you, I thought you will not understand my situation, but thank you, you showed me so much, love. I am going away, the Lord is waiting for me, and I see God and Jesus on his right hand, I see his glory."

All of us will die one day, it is a question of where we will go after we have died. Are you willing to risk a lifetime of torment in Hell and the lake of fire? Once you enter Hell or even the lake of fire, there is no coming back to this earth again. After what I have shared in this book, will you still insist, "I will believe unless I have seen?"

My appeal to you is do not put off believing and repenting for another day. You are alive at this moment, but there is no guarantee that you will be alive in the next five seconds. And what happened if you died yesterday, or even ten minutes ago? Where will you be?

Every minute or second, we live in unbelief, and we live in open sin or with secret sins, we face the danger of going to Hell. It is God's mercy that you are alive today. Think about all your friends or family or even colleagues who have died, were they prepared for such a final hour?

My aim in sharing my out-of-body experience is not to scare you into believing, God does not want ignorant believers, but he wants people to understand his word, and believe the truth, for God's word is the truth.

"For what shall profit a man, if he gains the whole world, and yet lose his own life" Mark 8: 36. Jesus asked this question to a crowd of people which included his disciples. This question is still relevant today. By the soul, Jesus meant the inner person. The body is just a container in which the soul [inner person] dwells, only the soul is everlasting, the body and all material possessions and wealth are temporal, and they fade with time, but the soul lives forever.

People spend all their time seeking to acquire wealth and material possessions. This busyness blinds them and occupies their time and energies so that they neglect the soul. You cannot compare the soul and material possessions and wealth; the value of your soul cannot be equal to anything in the world.

Yet, the pursuit of wealth and material possessions makes us neglect what is of infinite value, "love not the world, neither the things that are in the world. If any man loves the world, the love of the Father is not in him. For all that is the world, the lust of the flesh, and the lust of the eyes, the pride of life, is not of the Father but is of this world. The world passes away, the lust thereof: but he that does the will of God abides forever" 1 John 2: 15-17.

I had an elderly friend who passed away thirteen years ago, the man was a source of inspiration and wisdom to me. One day he told me a sad story about his life. He said, "I spent all my time and energy in search of money and material things, my wife and I were extremely ambitious, we wanted comfort and luxury to an extent that we forgot the most important thing we were supposed to do, that is having children of our own. Today am old and dying, having money and material things would not make up for not having children of my own, and dying with no heir of mine to give all these things I have gained in life is the source of constant pain to me."

The man asked me to be an heir and inherit all his money and material things which he had, but I refused, and instead suggested that he choose his nephew to be his heir.

The story of my elderly friend taught me this lesson; we can work all our lives to gain money and material things, only to find out that as we near the end of our lives, those things [money and wealth] do not matter. We can miss what is tremendously important in this life, the soul especially, and most importantly, it is the real self, and the soul of a person does not cease to exist.

What kept my elderly friend from what is important in life was the pursuit of business, you know business can keep you busy and occupy you to an extent that you miss the most important things in life, nothing can compensate for the loss of your soul, your soul is the real you, and is of infinite value.

At the end of his life, he found out he had missed what was especially important, you can also find out that at the end of your life, you have lost the opportunity to save your life.

Before I got out of my body for 30 minutes, I had occupied myself with studying, work, and pleasure. I was an ambitious man; I had so much wanted to be a rich man and live a luxurious life. All these kept me from seeking the salvation of my soul, had God not been merciful to me, by allowing me back into my body again, I will be in Hell suffering pain and torment for many years now.

God did not allow me back into my body so that I can continue living the same lifestyle I lived before, that God added more years to my life means that he has an assignment for me. And this assignment includes sharing the testifying about my life so that many people might be saved through my testimony.

You are alive and healthy; it is not your health or even your regular exercises that keep you alive and healthy. Many of your peers have died, some from long illnesses, but others have died suddenly without any sickness or health complications.

Who is keeping you alive? You could have died yesterday and gone to Hell to suffer pain and torment, but God is keeping you alive. But you are not even sensible about that, you are like an unproductive tree in the garden. God is giving you his rain, sunshine, and air, but you have not shown gratitude for his provisions, you have continued in sin without remorse.

My prayer is that the Holy Spirit will use this book to convince you the reader that you may know that you are a sinner and in the hands of the angry judge. "For the wrath of God is revealed from heaven against all ungodliness and unrighteousness of men who hold the truth in unrighteousness" Romans 1: 18.

Many preachers speak about the love and mercy of God in Christ but seldom speak about the anger of God. We find it difficult to speak about the angry God and loving and merciful God in the same breath. We think God is like us, "these things have done, and I kept silence; you thought that I was altogether such as yourself: but I will rebuke you and set them in order before your eyes" Psalms: 50: 21.

When God is silent, we think either he does not see or know about our evil deeds. We find it hard to stay angry with people we love, it is easier to be harsh or even act cruelly to people we do not love but indulge in people we love.

God is nothing like us, he punishes those he loves, "for whom the Lord loves he chastens, and scourges every son whom he receives" Hebrews 12: 6. Most people rightly say, "God is love", but are wrong to conclude that since God is love, he will not send anyone to Hell.

Both the righteousness and the wrath of God are revealed, the wrath is revealed because man is an unrighteous sinner who needs the righteousness of God, man is guilty before, and he is guilty because he has broken God's law, therefore deserves to go to Hell to suffer torment as the punishment for breaking the law of God.

God is angry with sinners, "to me belongs vengeance and recompense; their foot shall slide in due time: for the day of their calamity is at hand, and the things that shall come upon them make haste" Deuteronomy 32: 35. A sinner is like someone walking in a slippery place, and without being pushed, he is liable to fall on his own. God does not need to even punish a sinner, sin on its own is destructive.

About the Author

Martin Ndlovu is a graduate and former lecturer at Evangelical College of western Australia in South Africa. Martin is a passionate evangelist, and as an evangelist, he has been collaborating with men and women of God to bring the Good news to people who do not know God.

Martin is the husband of Mpho Ndhlovu, and a father to four children, [two sons and daughters]; Pule, Risuna, Kamohelo, and Tintswalo.

In case you want to communicate with Martin, you can write an email to martinndhlovu2019@gmail.com